WINNING
WITH
100

BEST OF THE BEST
PROMOTIONS

THE REGGIE AWARD WINNERS

PROMOTION MARKETING ASSOCIATION OF AMERICA, INC.

PROMOTION
POWER

DARTNELL is a publisher serving the world of business with books, manuals, newsletters and bulletins, and training materials for executives, managers, supervisors, salespeople, financial officials, personnel executives, and office employees. Dartnell also produces management and sales training videos and audiocassettes, publishes many useful business forms, and many of its materials and films are available in languages other than English. Dartnell, established in 1917, serves the world's business community. For details, catalogs, and product information, write or phone:

THE DARTNELL CORPORATION
4660 N Ravenswood Ave
Chicago, IL 60640-4595
(800) 621-5463 (in U.S. and Canada)

This publication is designed to provide accurate and authoritative information in regard to the subject matter covered. It is sold with the understanding that the publisher is not engaged in rendering legal, accounting, or other professional service. If legal advice or other expert assistance is required, the services of a competent professional person should be sought.

—From a Declaration of Principles jointly adopted by a Committee of the American Bar Association and a Committee of Publishers.

THE DARTNELL CORPORATION
4660 N Ravenswood Ave
Chicago, IL 60640-4595
Phone: (312) 561-4000
Fax: (312) 561-3801
Toll Free: (800) 621-5463
Speakers Bureau: (800) 545-7550

DARTNELL MARKETING PUBLICATIONS
286 Congress St
6th Floor
Boston, MA 02210
Phone: (617) 451-7551
Fax: (617) 451-8149
Toll Free: (800) 468-3038

DARTNELL TRAINING LIMITED
125 High Holborn
London, England
WC1V 6QA
Phone: 011-44-071-404-1585
Fax: 011-44-071-404-1580

©1994 The Dartnell Corporation
ISBN 0-85013-230-4
Library of Congress Catalog Card Number: 93-74412
Printed in the USA by The Dartnell Press

PREFACE

Imagine this. *Winning with Promotion Power* as required reading for a Ph.D. in promotion marketing.

Depending on your perspective, the distance between imagination and reality might be measured in one of two ways. The first "milepost" is the lack of a Ph.D. program in promotion marketing. Of course, there's also no master's program, no four-year degree—not even a minor or emphasis program. (Kind of odd, considering that the promotion marketing discipline commands three out of every four marketing dollars.)

But here's the second paradox, often heard as a generic criticism: "The Reggies, like all of these award programs, is a sort of business beauty contest. It has no place in serious education."

The truth of the first statement makes a lie out of the second. The validation is simple. If you are reading this, you are likely involved in some way in the promotion marketing discipline. Ask yourself, where did you acquire the tools of your trade? If you're like most of us, the answer lies somewhere between the files of your predecessor and the seat of your pants.

So, if awards programs are good learning tools, what's so special about the Reggies? Simple answer, again.

For the last five years, I've had the pleasure of observing the Reggie judging process. For a decade or so before that, I've been part of this business. I've also been a judge for other similar programs.

The Reggies is the only program that I have seen that bears no ties to private interests or publications. Sponsored by the Promotion Marketing Association of America, Inc., (PMAA) this award program is dedicated solely to the promotion marketing industry to measure and honor the best promotions using state-of-the-art standards.

The judges in the Reggie competition are seasoned promotion professionals who recognize the difference between an attractive campaign and an effective promotion. Read, for example, the 1990-1991 Colgate/Warner-Lambert tie-in promotion, (page 158). Some might see it as kind of boring, until one really looks at the objectives and, especially, the implementation. That's marketing art and science at its best!

So, your personal mandate is to ignore your "beauty pageant" prejudices. Read first the marketing objectives of these winners, almost ignoring the product or the advertising. How did that Reggie winner meet the objective? You'll see a whole new world open up in front of you. Brand building was never so good.

Speaking of brand building, books like this are usually the product of a consortium effort. I'm pleased to acknowledge the extraordinary work of Emilie Lion of the PMAA staff; the editorial, art, and production staff at the publisher, Dartnell; Rich Hagle, formerly of Dartnell; and Donna Howard and Fran Caci of Promotional Resources Group, who championed the project.

Read, enjoy, and prosper.

—Christopher J. Sutherland
Executive Director
Promotion Marketing Association of America, Inc.

INTRODUCTION

This book is about promotion marketing. It contains the case histories of some of the very best promotion marketing programs of the past decade. And, for most books about a multibillion dollar business subject, that would be sufficient. But promotion marketing (or sales promotion, as it has been more commonly known) is different. Although it is probably the world's oldest and most prominent form of mass selling, promotion marketing has also been the least understood, most poorly defined until recent years, and the least appreciated. In many companies promotion budgets have surpassed advertising budgets, but promotion neither carries the prestige of advertising nor receives the recognition.

"Mere lagniappe," sniffed an editorial writer more than a century ago in response to a premium offer for a product of the last part of the 19th century. That writer may have disdained lagniappe — offering the purchaser small, inexpensive gifts to encourage a larger order. But the practice engenders such goodwill that it is virtually ubiquitous to sales, and its roots stretch back to the dawn of mercantile civilization.

Athenian idol merchants offered premiums of incense, lamps, and drinking cups to buyers. Ladies of ancient Rome could receive the magic tooth of a Hyrcanian wolf mounted in gold to ensnare an unsuspecting lover. It was "gift-with-purchase" offered by cosmetics vendors.

The importance of promotion marketing has grown during the past two decades for several reasons. First, when properly planned and executed, promotion marketing can work better than any form of marketing communication — alone or in a mix with other forms. Second, it produces results sooner than other forms of marketing communication. The cases in this book provide testimony to the first point. The second is supported by any number of research studies and reports in the business press that promotion now accounts for as much as 70 percent of the total advertising and marketing communications expenditures of most companies. Third, the efforts of organizations such as the Promotion Marketing Association of America, Inc. (PMAA) bring greater professionalism to the industry. And this book is just one piece of evidence to support the success of these efforts.

What is promotion marketing?

In recent years, as promotion marketing has gained prominence and recognition as an effective marketing technique, many individuals and organizations have attempted to define it. Most of these attempts have emphasized promotion marketing as playing an ancillary or supplemental role. The PMAA, the organization that has been in the forefront of developing professionalism in the industry, defines it as:

> *An element in the marketing mix designed to stimulate consumer action*
> *and/or dealer effectiveness through various incentives.*

Analyzing the elements of this definition shows its thoroughness in the way it combines the simplicity and complexity of the field:

1. As "an element in the marketing mix," the promotion marketing portions of campaigns often support larger efforts. But as cases in this book show, that role is changing. In many programs the promotional elements are actually the driving force, while support comes from other elements, such as radio or television advertising. Most important here is the implicit recognition that marketing programs are synergistic efforts employing several disciplines. Promotion marketing elements work well with all elements of the marketing mix.

2. "To stimulate consumer action" is the key reason behind promotion marketing's increased usage and popularity. Unlike advertising, which can produce many positive long-term results, promotion marketing techniques help a potential purchaser decide to buy now rather than at some undefined time in the future. The results of promotion marketing are actions that can be measured.

3. "Dealer effectiveness" points up the range of promotion marketing effectiveness. Unlike other marketing communication techniques, promotion marketing programs can be (and often are) integrated throughout the entire chain, from the manufacturer to the consumer. Marketers aren't forced to choose between traditional "push" or "pull" strategy: Every player along the path to the final purchase and purchaser can be energized and incentivized to get behind the product and to make the sale.

4. "Various incentives" again points to the flexibility of promotion marketing devices. The biggest winners, which are cited in this book, didn't necessarily give the biggest incentives. Rather, they tailored their offers to address their immediate marketing challenges and the demands of their consumers.

What are the Reggies?

By the early 1980s promotion marketing had exploded. The use of various techniques was increasing exponentially each year. Professional marketers were looking for standards of excellence to train newcomers to the field, to convince others in their organizations of the valuable uses of promotional techniques, and to recognize individuals and organizations that had achieved outstanding success. In 1983, as the leading association in the field, the PMAA launched the Reggies: a series of awards to identify and honor the best promotional programs of the year.

The name of the award — The Reggie — is derived from "cash register." It was chosen because "nothing happens until a sale is made."

Judging criteria

As with any new venture, there are stages of conception, development, trial, and error before success can truly be realized. Such was the case of the early years when judging criteria were being established.

The first year (1983-1984) the Reggie Awards honored promotions by category. Effective execution received the most emphasis. The judges relied heavily on the visuals, and the entry form required only top-line information. In the second year (1984-1985), categories were eliminated and the entry form required more detailed information. With additional refinements, the entry form and judging criteria established in 1985-1986 closely resemble those used today.

The years 1983-1984 through 1987-1988 saw Reggies distributed on two levels: gold as first place, and silver as second place. But by 1988-1989, the high quality of many entries made it increasingly difficult for the judges to decipher between first-place and second-place programs. Thus, all winners from that point on were awarded the gold standard. The differences in criteria for the earlier years mean that the earlier case studies may be less comprehensive than the later ones. But all are outstanding sources of ideas and "hands-on" use of promotion marketing techniques.

Here are the established criteria for judging entries:

Ten winning entries are selected based on originality, execution, and results as a solution to the stated objectives of the program. In determining originality, judges consider the uniqueness of the promotion concept, innovation in strategy and tactics, and any executional elements that exhibit an appropriate approach to the promotion objectives. In examining execution, judges weigh clarity of the tactics and how well they were communicated to the target audience. Quantitative results must be included and are judged on the basis of the ability to demonstrate the promotion's effectiveness in achieving a goal that is compatible with the promotion's stated objectives.

The judging panel itself consists of a group of no less than seven and no more than 11 individuals whose professional backgrounds include several years of related promotion marketing experience. Judges are selected to reflect as broad a representation of the industry as possible, from both the agency and the marketer sides, and from as broad a sampling of industries as possible.

All entrants are required to submit program information on a case history form that includes:

1. Participants (company and agency, if applicable)
2. Background of the company and the product(s) involved
3. Detailed explanation of the marketing problem
4. Statement of objectives
5. Complete explanation of the program, including tactics used to execute the program
6. Results. In many cases this information is proprietary, but at least benchmark comparisons must be given.

In addition to the basic criteria, various judges have mentioned two ancillary specific criteria:

1. The presentation of the entry itself
2. The execution, reflected in the results.

A clear, concise presentation of the entry itself is the first step to engaging the judges' attention.

Execution of the promotion program, as reflected in the results, is especially important because it leads to success or failure. Programs most often come up short on execution. Even more than great strategy or great creative ideas, great execution is vital. Marketing professionals have become more adept at creating promotional programs, which has increased the challenge for the judges to select winners, but the Reggies are truly the "best of the best."

How the Reggies can help: What you can learn

Because the Reggie award winners do, in fact, represent the "best of the best" in promotion marketing for a particular year, reading and considering their implications carefully can provide several benefits.

First, they are presented in a case study format. Information is in-depth, yet compact and to the point. They provide a convenient, familiar way to gain insights into how the winners achieved their success. Second, the broad cross-section of fields represented by the winners provides a wide range of promotion strategies, tactics, executions, and applications. Different product categories use techniques that are new and different from other categories.

Third, the one key criterion for winning is results, which means that the promoter was able to identify and appeal to those things that most motivated the consumer and/or the trade/sales force. Thus, the cases offer valuable insight into consumer and trade/sales force motivations.

Finally, the cases are an excellent source of ideas so that the readers can use them to promote their own products. The tendency might be to read only those case studies that relate to a specific field or product. But there may be many good ideas commonly executed in other fields that have not been used in your field. Read all the case studies — and read them with an open mind. Say to yourself, "How can I apply anything in this program to what my needs are? How can I add a twist to an element to make it appropriate?" The specific information regarding program execution can provide the kind of insight that can spell success. While some of the winners executed truly unique programs, many winners used tried-and-true methods that have been used both successfully and unsuccessfully in the past by hundreds of marketers. The difference was the execution, as is apparent from reading the cases.

How to use this book

The organization of this book is simple and straightforward. Winners from the years 1983 to 1993 are listed in chronological order. Individual entries are organized by:

- Name of winner
- Name of program
- Background/marketing problem
- Statement of objectives
- The program-strategy/tactics
- The results.

This book's organization has one unique feature: Index 1. Unlike traditional indexes, it is organized as a "product-promotion" grid. The grid lists the winners down the left-hand margin. Across the top are the various kinds of promotion marketing techniques. For each promotion, the techniques used are listed, with the primary technique so indicated. The effect of the whole is to provide a highly usable "snapshot" of all techniques employed over the years, and their relative importance in overall promotion programs.

Trends in promotion marketing

Promotion marketing is such a broad field that it is difficult to make global statements about trends from such a small sampling as the Reggie winners. However, a close look at the grid, in addition to comments by the judges, who have also seen hundreds of very good promotions that did not make the final selection, does show some definite patterns.

Most significant in terms of strategy is the continued effort to get closer to the trade as well as to the consumer. This has translated into greater retailer emphasis in promotion planning and program development. Because the retailer is closest to the consumer buying decision in most categories, this makes retailer involvement crucial to the success of most promotion programs. In an overwhelming number of programs "increase retailer display activity" was a stated objective and, in some cases, this goal led to an account-specific program.

The need to control costs and to maximize impact has translated into a greater number of multiple product and tie-in promotions to leverage borrowed interest. Companies have always attempted to find synergies within their own product lines, but recent years have witnessed increased cooperation between multiple companies producing very different kinds of products that have only one thing in common, but it is the most important: the buyer or end-user. Of the 100 plus case studies in this publication, almost half involved an association with another company, a theatrical, sports, or charitable event.

In the more recent years, the degree of sophistication in promotional execution has increased dramatically. We are seeing a variety of techniques and technological elements, such as telemarketing, talking products, and interactive displays. In several instances, these newer approaches were actually the driving force of the promotion. Similarly, more and more videos are being incorporated into programs, not only targeted to the consumer, but also to the trade and sales force, especially for sales training. Sweepstakes have become less and less the focus of a promotion, but rather an overlay to the various other elements or techniques. Some of these trends are directly reflected in the product-promotion grid; others are not. By looking at the grid one can see the specific movement. The check marks indicating kinds of techniques used move farther and farther to the right.

On the other hand, such traditional techniques as refunding, premiums, and couponing are alive and well and visible in most programs.

In summary, marketers now realize that promotion, as well as advertising, can build brand equity. All of which leads to one final comment about trends and the future: Effective promotion marketing has become basic to the marketing success of nearly any product, regardless of financial constraints and changing technology. And here, in this book, are the very best examples of how it can work for your product.

—THE EDITORS

TABLE OF CONTENTS

TABLE OF CONTENTS

TABLE OF CONTENTS

TABLE OF CONTENTS

1983-1984

REGGIE

AWARDS

CAMPAIGNS

WIN MORE THAN A GREAT VACATION — YAMAHA MOTOR CORPORATION AND ADIDAS

MICKEY'S CHRISTMAS CASH REFUND OFFER — THE COCA-COLA COMPANY

BUSCH CASSIDY AND THE RAINDANCE KID IN THE GREAT POKER SHOOT OUT
— ANHEUSER-BUSCH, INC.

SPRING BREAK '83 — ANHEUSER-BUSCH, INC.

DEL MONTE COUNTRY FAIR — DEL MONTE CORPORATION

TIDY CAT³ DE-CAT-LON GAME — LOWE'S INC.

BRING AMERICA HOME SWEEPSTAKES — GENERAL ELECTRIC COMPANY

WORKMATES SWEEPSTAKES — THE TIMBERLAND COMPANY

WHO KILLED THE ROBINS FAMILY? CONTEST — WILLIAM MORROW & CO., INC.

LOOK LIKE A MILLION, LIVE LIKE A MILLION SWEEPSTAKES — REVLON

GET 'EM WHILE THEY'RE HOT WHEELS — MCDONALD'S

FREE 30 MINUTES OF LONG-DISTANCE CALLS — MCI TELECOMMUNICATIONS CORP.

B&B HOLIDAY GIFT GIVING — BENEDICTINE MARKETING SERVICES

ORVILLE REDENBACHER/MICKEY'S CHRISTMAS CAROL — HUNT WESSON FOODS, INC.

GIVE A GIFT, GET A GIFT — THE SPERRY & HUTCHINSON CO. INC.

BONANZA BANK INCENTIVE PROGRAM — SCOTT PAPER COMPANY

1983-84

CAMPAIGN/EVENT

Win More Than A Great Vacation

COMPANY

Yamaha Motor Corporation/Adidas

BRAND

Yamaha Riva Motorscooter

AGENCY

The Howard Marlboro Group

YEAR/AWARD

1983-84/1st Place

CATEGORY

Automotive

OBJECTIVES

- Introduce and create consumer awareness for the Riva motorscooter.
- Position the Riva as a vehicle used by affluent, sports-oriented audiences and remove the motorcycle image.

PROGRAM/STRATEGY

In order to help achieve these objectives, Yamaha developed a sweepstakes that tied-in to two upscale, tennis-oriented companies...Adidas and Hilton Head, both of which provided exposure for the Riva on nontraditional levels.

The sweepstakes, which was delivered via point of sale and magazine ads, provided the ideal vehicle for delivering the exact target audience that Yamaha wanted to reach.

Adidas, a national leader in tennis and sports merchandise, provided lower-level sweepstakes prizes. Adidas also displayed the Riva in selected stores and provided point of sale at participating stores. Hilton Head, the prestigious tennis resort and community, provided Yamaha with a memorable grand prize for the sweepstakes—a pro tournament at Hilton

Head. The host pro, Stan Smith, served as spokesperson for the Riva and, through letters under his name, recruited participation and support of the major pro shops for the promotion.

RESULTS

The promotion was considered successful in that it obtained the following results:

- More than 15,000 sweepstakes entries were received from 500,000 magazine entry forms and 5,000 point-of-sale locations.
- Yamaha achieved high awareness of the Riva for attractiveness and availability among the designated tennis audience, as measured by a pre/post study.
- Riva dealers requested that the program be repeated.

1983-84

CAMPAIGN/EVENT
Mickey's Christmas Cash Refund Offer

COMPANY
The Coca-Cola Company

BRAND
Coca-Cola

AGENCY
Don Jagoda Associates

YEAR/AWARD
1983-84/1st Place Tie

CATEGORY
Beverages

OBJECTIVES

- Generate store traffic and consumer purchase of Coca-Cola during the holiday season.
- Secure bottler participation.

PROGRAM/STRATEGY

With the purchase of Coca-Cola products consumers were able to receive two different booklets containing more than $500 in refund and rebate offers for a variety of holiday gift items.

A tie-in with The Walt Disney Company provided the theme for the promotion and featured Mickey in costume from the release of "Mickey's Christmas Carol," as well as TV and magazine print support.

The promotion was supported nationally through extensive advertising and locally through point-of-sale materials.

RESULTS

The program achieved 60 percent bottler participation covering more than 75 percent of the United States.

1983-84

CAMPAIGN/EVENT
Busch Cassidy and The Raindance Kid in the Great Poker Shoot-Out

COMPANY
Anheuser-Busch, Inc.

BRAND
Busch Beer

AGENCY
Focus Marketing, Inc.

YEAR/AWARD
1983-84/1st Place Tie

CATEGORY
Beverages

OBJECTIVES

- Generate brand awareness and visibility in the young adult market.
- Increase consumption.
- Reinforce western image advertising in a contemporary manner.
- Generate trade enthusiasm.

PROGRAM/STRATEGY

In selected college newspapers, Busch ran a poster puzzle featuring five characters each with a hand of poker with two cards revealed for each hand. A clue ran with the puzzle along with subsequent clues at weekly intervals. The objective was to determine who had the winning hand of poker. An 800 number was utilized to call in the solutions. One winner from each was selected to receive the prize of a Florida vacation during spring break.

The same materials were used at retail to involve the trade.

RESULTS

Research suggested that the Great Poker Shoot Out was the most successful sweepstakes in the brand's history on the basis of awareness, involvement, and entry levels.

1983-84

CAMPAIGN/EVENT
Spring Break '83

COMPANY
Anheuser-Busch, Inc.

BRAND
Budweiser Beer

AGENCY
Focus Marketing, Inc.

YEAR/AWARD
1983-84/1st Place Tie

CATEGORY
Beverages

OBJECTIVES

- Position Budweiser preemptively as "the" beer of today's young adult lifestyle.
- Create a larger-than-life spring break image for Budweiser beers.

PROGRAM/STRATEGY

Budweiser created the "Spring Break Guide," which provided information for college students about the most popular spring break vacation sites and other useful details about those locales. The "Guide" was delivered to its target audience of college students, via campus newspapers, which gave Budweiser the opportunity to reach not only those who were going on spring break but also carried the Budweiser image to 90 percent of the students not physically attending spring break. Budweiser took a basic event, the spring break, and through a special event campaign and imaginative programs such as Can Exchange, live concerts, and poolside parties, turned it into a national promotion to provide a compelling point of difference from its competitors.

RESULTS

Budweiser achieved exceptional media coverage both in-market and across the United States as well as major support from city officials whose communities were supported through the "Spring Break Guide." By successfully preempting the category, the program has been destined to become a Budweiser tradition.

1983-84

CAMPAIGN/EVENT

Del Monte Country Fair

COMPANY

Del Monte Corporation

BRAND

Del Monte Canned and Processed Foods

YEAR/AWARD

1983-84/1st Place

CATEGORY

Grocery Products

OBJECTIVES

- Stimulate consumer interest in purchasing Del Monte products.
- Support strategic "growth" for specific products in selected markets.
- Generate trade support.

PROGRAM/STRATEGY

Reinforcing the product line of vegetables and fruits, Del Monte developed the Country Yumkins, a line of plush character fruits and vegetables. Eight different Yumkins with a retail value of $15 each were offered free in the mail for multiple proofs-of-purchase.

RESULTS

Nearly 400,000 Yumkins were sent out, resulting in the collection of more than 25 million product labels.

1983-84

CAMPAIGN/EVENT

Tidy Cat3 De-Cat-Lon Game

COMPANY

Lowe's Inc.

BRAND

Tidy Cat3 Kitty Litter

AGENCY

Einson Freeman, Inc.

YEAR/AWARD

1983-84/1st Place Tie

CATEGORY

Household Goods

OBJECTIVES

- Generate incremental volume through consumer excitement.
- Obtain trade merchandising support.

PROGRAM/STRATEGY

For the first time in this category, an in-pack game, the Tidy Cat3 De-Cat-Lon, was utilized. The theme was chosen to capitalize on the upcoming Winter Olympic Games without the cost of sponsorship. Game cards had 10 events cleverly structured to mimic sports events such as litter boxing, scratch pole vaulting, etc. Consumers scratched off any three of the 10 events to uncover winning threesomes. Every card had a match either for a free reflector medal for cats or cash prizes ranging up to $33,333...playing off the Tidy Cat3 name.

A trade sweepstakes, the Profit Pentathlon, was also included, offering free carloads of product as a trade prize.

RESULTS

Tidy Cat3 experienced a volume increase during the promotion period as the event outperformed the strongest promotion in the brand's history.

1983-84

CAMPAIGN/EVENT
Bring America Home Sweepstakes

COMPANY
General Electric Company

BRAND
GE Videos

AGENCY
Marcon Marketing Services

YEAR/AWARD
1983-84/1st Place Tie

CATEGORY
Household Goods

OBJECTIVES

- Build dealer traffic and increase sales over previous year's sales.
- Increase product mix.
- Enhance technological image.

PROGRAM/STRATEGY

A sweepstakes was developed offering a high-technology vehicle: a Video Explorer van equipped with GE video components, appliances, and a satellite receiving system, as the grand prize. The van was made available to dealers for store showings as a means of building traffic, awareness, and trade involvement.

The program was supported by a full-page, four-color advertisement in Sunday supplements as well as point-of-sale materials with entry forms.

RESULTS

The promotion was judged to be the direct cause of a 10 percent increase in sales over the previous year. The promotion contributed to new distribution gains and to the successful building awareness of GE's video products.

1983-84

CAMPAIGN/EVENT

Workmates Sweepstakes

COMPANY

The Timberland Company

BRAND

Timberland boots

AGENCY

Burke Promotional Marketing

YEAR/AWARD

1983-84/1st Place Tie

CATEGORY

Personal Accessories

OBJECTIVES

- Generate increased awareness and market share for work boots during the Winter/Christmas season.
- Develop retailer support and increase inventories on work boots.
- Motivate sales force.

PROGRAM/STRATEGY

An in-store sweepstakes was developed with a winner every two weeks in all participating stores. Winners could choose a Black & Decker prize that "worked best for them." Point-of-sale displays contained a Black & Decker work center which also served as a dealer loader.

A retail sales force incentive program was also implemented awarding a free work shirt and boots for incremental sales.

The program was supported with full-page ROP ads with dealer listings as well as local TV commercials.

RESULTS

Sales versus the same period of the previous year increased 300 percent and market share increased 33 percent.

1983-84

CAMPAIGN/EVENT

Who Killed The Robins Family? Contest

COMPANY

William Morrow & Co., Inc.

BRAND

Who Killed The Robins Family?, a novel

AGENCY

Ventura Associates

YEAR/AWARD

1983-84/1st Place Tie

CATEGORY

Personal Accessories

OBJECTIVE

• Create a major consumer event by generating media coverage and sales of a mystery novel by an unknown author.

PROGRAM/STRATEGY

For the first time in this category in the United States, Ventura introduced a contest that encouraged consumers to solve a murder mystery and answer five questions pertaining to the murder in the novel. A $10,000 reward was offered to the contestant who best solved the mystery. The solutions were to be part of a second publication entitled *The Revenge of the Robins Family.*

"Blood stained" displays, counter cards, and banners were used at point of sale. The contest was supported with advertisements in book reviews including *The New York Times Book Review.*

RESULTS

Who Killed The Robins Family? remained on *The New York Times* Best Seller List for 34 weeks and sold a number of copies far beyond the highest expectations. So unique was the concept that it received exceptional media coverage, including an in-depth article in *People* magazine and several talk show interviews with the author.

1983-84

CAMPAIGN/EVENT

Look Like a Million, Live Like a Million Sweepstakes

COMPANY

Revlon

BRAND

The Fall shades of cosmetics

YEAR/AWARD

1983-84/1st Place

CATEGORY

Personal Products

OBJECTIVES

- Support the introduction of Revlon's Million Dollar Colors—The Fall shades of color cosmetics.
- Increase store traffic.
- Generate excitement at the sales and trade level.

PROGRAM/STRATEGY

Revlon executed a sweepstakes with upscale prizes such as designer mink coats and diamond jewelry, along with a $1 million bonus prize. On a local level, Revlon teamed up with retailers to conduct local sweepstakes awarding mink jackets and diamond jewelry to local customers.

The program was supported by TV, print ads, and point-of-sale displays including sweepstakes entry forms.

RESULTS

Revlon oversold their prepacked merchandise projections by more than 12 percent. The campaign prize structure attracted coverage from all major networks and newspapers.

1983-84

CAMPAIGN/EVENT
Get 'Em While They're Hot Wheels

COMPANY
McDonald's Corporation

AGENCY
Frankel & Company

YEAR/AWARD
1983-84/1st Place

CATEGORY
Restaurants

OBJECTIVE

- The single objective was to increase sales and transactions.

PROGRAM/STRATEGY

A simple but very effective continuity offer of a popular premium at a popular price became the success story for this Reggie winner. With the purchase of any McDonald's food item, consumers could receive a Mattel Hot Wheels car at a special "hot" discounted price. A different car was offered every day with 14 different cars comprising the collection.

The program was supported with point of sale along with radio and TV.

RESULTS
Considered proprietary and cannot be published.

1983-84

CAMPAIGN/EVENT

Free 30 Minutes of Long-Distance Calls

COMPANY

MCI Telecommunications Corp.

BRAND

MCI Services

AGENCY

Burke Promotional Marketing

YEAR/AWARD

1983-84/1st Place

CATEGORY

Services

OBJECTIVES

- Increase residential subscriber base by 10 percent.
- Generate incremental sales.
- Improve telemarketing sales-to-force conversion rate.
- Increase awareness of MCI savings over AT&T systems.

PROGRAM/STRATEGY

MCI implemented the first major coupon offer by a telecommunications company. An FSI carried a coupon good for 30 free minutes of long-distance calls. Consumers redeemed their coupons by calling a toll-free number to sign up for MCI service.

RESULTS

The promotion generated 200,000 new customers which represented a 20 percent increase in the residential customer base.

1983-84

CAMPAIGN/EVENT
B&B Holiday Gift Giving

COMPANY
Benedictine Marketing Services

BRAND
B&B Liqueur

AGENCY
Marlboro Marketing Inc.

YEAR/AWARD
1983-84/2nd Place

CATEGORY
Beverages

OBJECTIVES

- Maintain promotional visibility and placement at retail.
- Increase sales during the holiday period.
- Satisfy the retailers' display needs at different levels.
- Obtain prominent counter position at small retailers.
- Command a dominant floor position in high-volume chains.

PROGRAM/STRATEGY

The objectives were met through the design of a unique in-store display. For the smaller stores the shipping vehicle converted into an instant holiday display for the six bottles inside. When opened the display also contained gift cards which were free to the consumer with purchase.

For chains, an 18-bottle display presented in embossed foil and full color became a focal point for in-store merchandising.

A prepacked counter unit containing 24 packages, each holding four minibottles, was designed to encourage impulse sales of a prestigious gift at a reasonable price.

RESULTS

The prominence of the displays resulted in a significant increase in holiday sales. Retailers responded favorably to the convenient displays and encouraged similar displays for other gift-giving periods.

1983-84

CAMPAIGN/EVENT

Orville Redenbacher/Mickey's Christmas Carol

COMPANY

Hunt Wesson Foods, Inc.

BRAND

Orville Redenbacher's Popcorns and Popping Oil

AGENCY

Joseph Potocki and Associates, Inc.

YEAR/AWARD

1983-84/2nd Place

CATEGORY

Grocery Products

OBJECTIVE

• The objective was to secure floor displays of this impulse item during the holiday season.

PROGRAM/STRATEGY

For an all-family impact, Hunt Wesson tied in the release of the first animated Disney movie in 37 years, "Mickey's Christmas Carol," with the purchase of Orville Redenbacher products.

The program offered a free coloring book from a near pack display. The coloring book was based on an abbreviated version of the movie.

The trade was given the opportunity to see the movie as Orville's guest.

RESULTS

The power of Mickey resulted in all-time high display activity during a very difficult period. Feature support exceeded the norm and share and consumption levels increased to an all-time record.

1983-84

CAMPAIGN/EVENT

Give A Gift, Get A Gift

COMPANY

The Sperry & Hutchinson Co. Inc.

BRAND

S&H Green Stamps

YEAR/AWARD

1983-84/2nd Place

CATEGORY

Services

OBJECTIVES

- Increase participating retailers' sales and profits by bringing in new customers and by increasing transaction size.
- Increase redemptions at S&H gift centers.

PROGRAM/STRATEGY

Focused around the Christmas gift-giving time, S&H distributed 6 million minicatalogs containing merchandise obtainable for S&H green stamps through direct mail. The catalogs were customized for 25 participating retailers by county and offered consumers a free gift when they redeemed S&H green stamps. The catalogs also contained coupons for various items which were redeemed by the retailers.

The program was supported with tags to existing S&H radio commercials and retailers ran drop-in newspaper ads to announce the mailer.

RESULTS

This partnership promotion with the retailers resulted in an average transaction size increase of more than 100 percent for participating retailers versus the national average. Coupon redemption exceeded estimated redemption by 100 percent and gift center redemptions were up 5 percentage points versus the prior year.

1983-84

CAMPAIGN/EVENT
Bonanza Bank Incentive Program

COMPANY
Scott Paper Company

BRAND
Scott Tissues

AGENCY
Don Jagoda Associates, Inc.

YEAR/AWARD
1983-84/2nd Place

CATEGORY
Personal Products

OBJECTIVES

- Motivate the Scott sales force, distributor salespeople, principals, and sales management.
- Increase sales and sales "push" for Scott products to both current and new distributors and their customers in a cost-efficient manner.

PROGRAM/STRATEGY

Scott created a multilevel incentive program with periodic sweepstakes offers using the theme of a prize Bonanza Bank with monthly savings account statements mailed to each participant. Distributor salespeople and sales managers earned Scott Bucks redeemable for items in the Bonanza Bank catalog. Based on sales quotas, Scott Bucks earnings could double. Regionally, distributor principals and Scott salespeople competed to win prizes based on percentage increases in sales. Distributor salespeople and sales managers received game cards which enabled them to win an interest dividend in Scott Bucks or merchandise prizes instantly.

RESULTS

This program successfully achieved the following:
- It generated an increase in sales (80+ percent of distributors achieved or exceeded their quotas).
- It enabled Scott to more effectively communicate with and motivate their distributor sales forces.
- It provided a basic incentive program that would be restructured and executed again in 1984.

1984-1985

REGGIE

AWARDS

CAMPAIGNS

WHEN THE U.S. WINS, YOU WIN — MCDONALD'S CORPORATION

MICHELOB WHOLESALER TURNKEY PROMOTION — ANHEUSER-BUSCH, INC.

ORVILLE REDENBACHER'S 'MATCH MY BOWTIE' CONTEST — HUNT WESSON FOODS, INC.

COMPUTERRIFIC SWEEPSTAKES — PROCTER AND GAMBLE AND IBM*

MAXWELL HOUSE INSTANT COFFEE ORNAMENT SPECIAL PACK — GENERAL FOODS CORPORATION

GO FOR THE GOLD PROGRAM — CAMPBELL SOUP COMPANY

GREAT TOGETHER — A&W BRANDS

GREMLINS BACK-TO-SCHOOL PROMOTION — THE DOW CHEMICAL COMPANY

"INDIANA JONES AND THE TEMPLE OF DOOM" GAME — THE SEVEN-UP COMPANY

WE WON'T GO BACK WITHOUT YOU — CORESCO, INC.

*PUBLICATION OF THE PROCTER & GAMBLE CASE STUDY IS RESTRICTED BY COMPANY POLICY.

1984-85

CAMPAIGN/EVENT
When The U.S. Wins, You Win

COMPANY
McDonald's Corporation

AGENCY
Simon Marketing, Inc. — Game; Leo Burnett Company — Advertising; and Frankel & Company — Point of Sale

YEAR/AWARD
1984-85/Gold/Super Reggie

BACKGROUND/MARKETING SITUATION

As the leader in the Fast Service Restaurant (FSR) category, McDonald's competed fiercely in the confrontational advertising milieu of the Burger Wars. As a major sponsor of the 1984 Summer Olympic Games, the chain executed an intrusive promotion to extend the impact of its TV advertising of the games.

OBJECTIVES

McDonald's objective was to benefit in a number of ways from its investment in the Olympics.
- To be the acknowledged leading sponsor of the 1984 Summer Games.
- To demonstrate leadership in the Quick Service Restaurant category without confrontational tactics.
- To increase store sales.
- To increase store transactions.
- To increase TV viewership of the 1984 Summer Games.

PROGRAM/STRATEGY

The strategy was to bring the fun and excitement of the Summer Games into every McDonald's store with a game that enabled customers to win a food prize whenever a member of the U.S. Olympic team won a medal. The game was titled McDonald's When the U.S. Wins, You Win! and its mechanics were easy and fun.

During the Summer Games, McDonald's distributed free game cards to everyone who came into a store. Each card had a rub-off spot. When the spot was rubbed off, the name of an Olympic event was revealed.

If the United States won a gold medal in the event, the holder of the card won a Big Mac sandwich. A silver medal won the holder an order of french fries, and a bronze medal won a soft drink. Grand prize was $10,000 cash.

Customers could play along with the Summer Games as they unfolded on television. Since Olympic medal winners were also posted daily in each store, customers had another reason to make a store visit to find out if they held the winning cards. They came back to get more game cards and to redeem their winning game cards.

RESULTS

The results of the McDonald's promotion were as follows:

- Participation levels by store owner/operator were the highest in McDonald's history.
- Total store sales increased.
- Store transactions increased.
- Average store sales were up in the six-week promotion period.
- McDonald's distributed more than 300 million game cards.
- McDonald's was recognized as the leading sponsor of the 1984 Summer Olympic Games.
- Through the combined impact of the promotion and advertising, the corporation's image among consumers improved significantly.

1984-85

CAMPAIGN/EVENT
Michelob Wholesaler Turnkey Promotion

COMPANY
Anheuser-Busch, Inc.

BRAND
Michelob Beer

AGENCY
Focus Marketing Inc.

YEAR/AWARD
1984-85/Gold

BACKGROUND/MARKETING SITUATION

Michelob, one of the Anheuser-Busch brands, ranked sixth in the marketplace. This beer was positioned as a top quality product, but despite advertising to support its premium image, it continued to languish in the shadow of its much larger sibling brand, Budweiser.

Michelob had limited promotional clout and was experiencing softness. Testing had identified an age-gap problem...the young adult segment was not responding to the beer's premium positioning and an important source of sales was consequently being forfeited. To correct the loss, funds originally earmarked for golf tournaments were redirected to this younger target and brand management would now have to develop an expeditious event.

OBJECTIVES

Expediency could not be achieved at the expense of appropriateness and brand image. Therefore, objectives were identified within the context of a mandate to avoid the kind of stereotyped imagery frequently employed by beer brands in the young adult market.

These objectives were to:
- Develop flexible promotions to fit both the college and working audiences.
- Reinforce the Michelob Some Things Speak For Themselves advertising campaign.

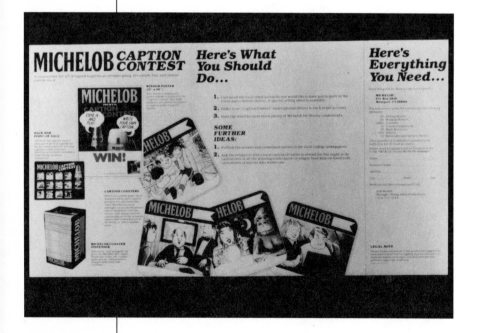

• Convince wholesalers to implement these promotions in their own markets.

PROGRAM/STRATEGY

To avert any further misdirection, Michelob brand management first enlisted the advice of young adults themselves who suggested that their age group identifies with "up-and-coming achievers."

Based on this data, a menu of eight promotions, each an easy-to-implement turnkey event, was mailed to each Michelob wholesaler with instructions to select the one event most applicable to that wholesaler's specific market.

One such event was the Michelob Caption Contest. The wholesaler received 10 coaster dispensers each filled with 400 Michelob coasters printed with amusing cartoons but lacking captions. The 10 retailers (in this case, college bars) were able to hold a Caption Contest Bar Night. Students could express their writing talents by writing captions directly on the coasters and submitting them as entries. The 12 coasters with the funniest captions could be displayed on a back-bar sign. Winners got free Michelob, recognition in college newspapers, and their own portrait cartoons drawn on the spot in the bar by local caricature artists.

RESULTS

This promotion elicited the highest percentage participation by A-B wholesalers in Michelob history. One event exceeded forecast by 60 percent. The "achiever" concept ultimately became the basis of a new thrust in Michelob's advertising strategy.

1984-85

CAMPAIGN/EVENT

Orville Redenbacher's Match My Bowtie Contest

COMPANY

Hunt Wesson Foods, Inc.

BRAND

Orville Redenbacher's Popcorns and Popping Oil

AGENCY

Joseph Potocki & Associates

YEAR/AWARD

1984-85/Gold

BACKGROUND/MARKETING SITUATION

In 1984, competition among popcorn brands in the snacks category was escalating. Hunt Wesson Foods was searching for a promotion event that would protect its Orville Redenbacher's popping corn and popping oil franchise. At the time, Orville Redenbacher's led in the jarred and microwave popping corn categories, as well as in popping oil.

OBJECTIVES

It was important to generate a point of difference that could break through the glut of consumer promotions and gain trade support, too.

CONSUMER

- Create an intrusive event to cut through clutter and gain awareness.
- Reinforce the Orville Redenbacher's advertising message.
- Increase consumption.
- Gain trial on new product line extensions.

TRADE

- Generate display activity.
- Continue brand momentum.
- Create a unique and memorable selling proposition.

PROGRAM/STRATEGY

An ingenious plan was developed to leverage the popularity of the brand spokesperson, Orville Redenbacher, in conjunction with consumer enthusiasm for Halloween and fall TV programming, two occasions when most popcorn is consumed.

A contest delivered right before Halloween via FSI and point-of-sale displays was designed to make consumers search for Orville Redenbacher's TV commercial ads. On the contest entry forms, consumers had to circle the bowtie that matched the tie worn by Orville in the commercials. First prize in the Match My Bowtie contest was a "trip for five to Hollywood to dine with Orville, tour TV studios, and visit with the stars." There were hundreds of lower-level prizes, too. To remind consumers of the brand's category leadership, the FSI boldly announced, "Prime Time TV is Orville Redenbacher's Time!"

To reinforce purchase and thus to attract trade support, each contest entry had to be accompanied by a proof of purchase from any Orville Redenbacher's product. In addition, two 20¢ coupons in the FSI encouraged multiple purchases. Strong trade allowances were offered to obtain feature and display support.

RESULTS

This promotion made the most of timing and brand image to boost consumption and share, thus keeping Orville Redenbacher's the leading name in the category. Display and feature support drove sales to a 38 percent increase over sales in the same period of the prior year.

1984-85

CAMPAIGN/EVENT

Maxwell House Instant Coffee Christmas Ornament Special Pack

COMPANY

General Foods Corporation

BRAND

Maxwell House Instant Coffee

YEAR/AWARD

1984-85/Gold

BACKGROUND/MARKETING SITUATION

Maxwell House Instant Coffee was the No.1 selling instant coffee in the nation from 1982 through 1984, and the brand was concerned about protecting its franchise. Recently, there had been several new product introductions from large competitors.

The marketing environment for coffee is volatile. Compounding the constant challenge imposed by competitor introductions, the industry relied heavily on couponing, and during fourth-quarter holidays retailers focused features on ground coffee, so trying to circumvent coupon clutter with alternate trade feature activity was also frustrating.

OBJECTIVES

Maxwell House Instant Coffee needed a unique fourth-quarter promotion proposition to achieve the following:

- Reduce consumer dependency on coupons as their incentive to purchase in high-franchise areas.
- Stimulate multiple purchases to insulate the franchise from promotion activity by key competitors.
- Maximize the brand's volume and share of market during the key holiday coffee merchandising period.

PROGRAM/STRATEGY

To reduce coupon dependency, the brand offered a free etched holiday ornament on-pack for added value. The holiday pack was attractively flagged and easy to recognize, thereby influencing consumers at the point of purchase. To encourage multiple purchases, three different ornaments were offered. Each was dated for collectibility. The pack was supported with coupons in low franchise areas.

This program began in 1982 as a test in two districts. The ornament was offered free with proofs-of-purchase via Carol Wright direct mail. An FSI and TV advertising supported the test.

In 1983 the on-pack program became national with a center-spread FSI, magazine ads, trade ads and extensive point of purchase material. In 1984, it expanded to include Maxwell House Ground Coffee in low franchise markets. In-store advertising and rotary displays were added.

RESULTS

The 1982 test boosted one district's share 118 percent, and key account acceptance of the holiday jar ranged from 77 percent to 87 percent.

The 1983 national program returned an average 3.8 percent in incremental share points. The ornament event proved to be 40 percent more effective and cost efficient than the average of the year's other consumer promotion events.

Results for the 1984 promotion were not available for reference when this case history was written but excitement was building again as consumers accumulated ornaments for their collections.

1984-85

CAMPAIGN/EVENT
Go For The Gold Program

COMPANY
Campbell Soup Company

BRAND
Campbell's Condensed Soups

YEAR/AWARD
1984-85/Silver

BACKGROUND/MARKETING SITUATION

Campbell's "red & white label" condensed soups were the leading brand in the prepared soup category in 1984. The line included more than 50 varieties of soups with more than 90+ percent distribution.

The prepared soup category encompasses condensed, ready-to-serve, and dry soups. The condensed segment was experiencing pressure from the ready-to-serve and dry segments, which had achieved large volume increases with new product introductions, heavy trade spending, and consumer trial incentives.

The approach of the 1984 Winter Olympic Games opened a window for Campbell's condensed soups to connect the Campbell's Soup Is Good Food campaign with the health and fitness perception surrounding the world's most prestigious winter sports event.

OBJECTIVES

This program would have to appeal to consumers, to the trade, and, internally, to the Campbell sales force. Objectives were to:
- Generate increased consumer usage rates and greater purchase continuity.
- Stimulate multiple purchase.
- Create trial of new and lesser volume soup varieties.
- Motivate retailers to tie-in to the Campbell's condensed soup varieties in each promotion schedule.
- Obtain feature pricing on one or more condensed soup varieties in each promotion period.
- Obtain in-store displays on promoted soup varieties.
- Maximize placement of merchandising materials in-store.
- Generate higher sales force productivity.

PROGRAM/STRATEGY

Campbell created an umbrella theme, Go For The Gold, that could engender a sense of immediacy but would maintain lasting awareness for the promotion schedule over four quarters. As the Official Soup of the 1984 Winter Olympic Games, more than 40 varieties of Campbell's condensed soups carried a message, "Official Soup—Winter Olympics," printed in blue and white on their labels to this effect.

A 12-month promotion schedule introduced one high volume product allowance per quarter, two consumer programs, Olympics themed mass media support, extensive Olympic Campbell Kid merchandising materials, and various themed incentives for consumers and the trade.

To pique consumer interest, in the summer of 1983, the consumer and trade incentives included self-liquidating offers for Go for the Gold sleeveless T-shirts and a Campbell's Soups pop art insulated bag for soda cans. Then in the fall, an FSI dropped featuring multiple-purchase coupons for five of the sponsoring soups. This consumer offer was followed by a Go for the Gold sweepstakes in February 1984, sponsored by Campbell's Vegetable Soups.

Throughout the duration of the program, :30 TV commercials appeared during prime time, daytime, and children's programming. One such spot featured Rosalyn Sumners of the U.S. Figure Skating Team. Network radio supplemented the TV schedule, while a series of full-color magazine ads ran in national and regional publications.

Perhaps the most appealing support materials were individual die cut standees of the Campbell's Kids as skiers, speed skaters, figure skaters, hockey players, and even as members of the bobsled team. Retailers could also order Olympics themed "Fuel for Fitness" case cards and shelf-talkers.

RESULTS

Consumer...Shipments increased by more than 30 million cans. Promoted varieties enjoyed yearlong increases in sales ranging from 4 percent to 8 percent.

Trade...More retailers tied-in than ever before in Campbell history. Feature pricing hit record highs in numbers of ads and in multiple price mentions. The combined events generated a 128 percent increase in trade features and a 148 percent increase in displays. More point-of-sale materials were produced and distributed than in any previous time in Campbell history.

Sales Force...Sales quotas were exceeded in each event and two of Campbell's highest volume soups were sold so extensively that no additional promotion was necessary for these varieties for the remainder of 1984.

1984-85

CAMPAIGN/EVENT
Great Together

COMPANY
A&W Brands

BRAND
A&W Root Beer

AGENCY
I.M. Towers & Company, Inc.

YEAR/AWARD
1984-85/Silver

BACKGROUND/MARKETING SITUATION

Among soft drinks, root beer was a paradoxical product. Nearly 75 percent of soft-drink consumers purchased root beer, and root beer generated nearly $1 billion in retail in 1984, yet root beer is considered an impulse purchase, and thus the category comprised only 4 percent of total soft-drink sales. During the peak summer season for soft drinks, root beer producers had to exert extraordinary promotion efforts to acquire support from bottlers and retailers.

A&W Root Beer was by far the largest-selling brand among root beers, yet it was sold by bottlers into retailers as a brand allied to one of the "big three"...Coca-Cola, Pepsi or 7-UP. Research showed that A&W sold 400 percent faster when it was displayed and featured.

OBJECTIVE

A&W Root Beer had one key goal for the summer...increase off-shelf displays and retail ad features.

PROGRAM/STRATEGY

The brand conceived a tie-in sale promoting A&W Root Beer and private label ice cream. The event celebrated that old-time favorite, the root beer float, and was themed to consumers and to the trade as "Great Together." The concept appealed to the self-interest of grocery chains with its potential to maximize profits through their own private label ice cream.

A&W enlisted the help of the International Association of Ice Cream Manufacturers. The association appointed A&W Root Beer to be its official soft drink. A&W national-accounts people supported the bottlers by making presentations for the event to both the beverage and dairy departments of each chain. Chains were given sell-in kits that emphasized the opportunity for increased profits. Trade publicity and ice cream industry presentations were so compelling that they prompted many chains themselves to approach bottlers to tie-in to the event.

Pole toppers for this event were especially creative and eye-catching. One highlighted a consumer self-liquidating offer for an A&W giant inflatable raft ("float"). The raft was also given to retailers in return for mass displays.

A second pole topper depicted a father and daughter sharing an A&W Root Beer float. These characters also appeared in TV advertising. The TV ads were the first such in the root beer industry to support a specific promotion.

Additional elements included cold case stickers, recipe neck hangers, take-one pads, and a float-making kit given away as a dealer loader. The Root Beer Float program showed A&W Root Beer bottlers how to tie a chain and an ice cream brand together for a successful sampling program.

RESULTS

Response went far beyond expectations. Eighteen of the 20 major national grocery chains utilized this event. Nielsen reported that A&W Root Beer volume rose 14 percent for June/July, while the soft-drink category rose only 1 percent and other root beers only 3 percent. Share for A&W Root Beer rose two share points.

At the trade level, displays were very successful. The float pole topper display forced a 210 percent display increase. A&W Root Beer ad feature penetration increased 23 percent to 53 percent.

In the end, this clever concept, firmly based on brand equity, careful research, and thorough execution, earned this event a place in the Reggies.

1984-85

CAMPAIGN/EVENT

Gremlins Back-To-School Promotion

COMPANY

The Dow Chemical Company

BRAND

Ziploc Sandwich Bags

YEAR/AWARD

1984-85/Silver

BACKGROUND/MARKETING SITUATION

In 1984 the sandwich bag category was growing at an annual rate of 6 percent, although case volume remained relatively stationary. The category was intensely competitive due to the influence of private label products. Ziploc Sandwich Bags ranked second in the category with a 28 percent share.

The back-to-school period, July through September, was the most active for the sandwich bag category and 35 percent of yearly volume was generated during these three months. Based on SAMI brand trends, Ziploc Sandwich Bags grew 2 percent when promoted for back-to-school but the brand had never achieved No. 1 share of market.

OBJECTIVES

Ziploc brand management understood that consumers looking for back-to-school bargains would rally to whichever sandwich bags the trade chose to support. They therefore set a goal to be the most promotable brand in the opinion of the trade during this period. Related goals were:

- Increase pre-packs placed by 26 percent versus 1983.
- Secure more feature ads from the trade than in 1983.
- Load the trade with product.
- Increase case volume by 26 percent versus 1983.
- Secure the No. 1 share of market in the sandwich bag category during the period.

PROGRAM/STRATEGY

A consumer program that would impress the trade was developed to include three vehicles:

- Free Gremlins stickers in specially marked Ziploc packages. There were two stickers per package and seven series of stickers to collect,

A Back-To-School Special from **Ziploc** Sandwich Bags

FREE BREAD

Receive by mail a coupon good for a free package of bread (up to $1.00 value) when you buy two packages of **Ziploc** brand Sandwich Bags, and any brand of bread.

Plus Free **GREMLiNS** Stickers
in specially marked packages of **Ziploc** brand Sandwich Bags

See the "Gremlins" movie at local theaters now!

Free Bread Offer Official Mail-In Certificate

featuring scenes from the current movie success "Gremlins."

- FSI drop carrying a 15¢ coupon.
- Mail-in offer for a free coupon for free bread (up to $1.00) with purchase of two Ziploc packages.

Trade objectives were achieved by offering the most complete promotional program in the category:

- Major national media drop.
- Allowances for feature ads.
- A special allowance for pre-pack placements.
- An overlay of national network TV ads.

RESULTS

The goals were reached and exceeded. Case sale volume rose 42 percent; pre-pack placement rose 40 percent; and operating margins rose 36 percent.

Most important, for the first time since its introduction, Ziploc Sandwich Bags realized the No. 1 position in the category.

1984-85

CAMPAIGN/EVENT

"Indiana Jones And The Temple Of Doom" Game

COMPANY

The Seven-Up Company

BRAND

7UP

AGENCY

Frankel & Company

YEAR/AWARD

1984-85/Silver

BACKGROUND/MARKETING SITUATION

In the soft drink industry, bottlers typically produce and sell the brands for more than one soft drink parent company in their franchise areas. Therefore, parent companies must jockey for bottler share of mind for their brands.

More than 70 percent of soft drink sales to consumers occur when products are on deal. This necessitates trade support with feature ads and displays. Consumers hold virtually no brand loyalty and will purchase the brand that offers best value.

In this environment, in 1984, 7UP ranked third overall and first among lemon-lime soft drinks. The key summer consumption period for 7UP was approaching.

OBJECTIVES

Objectives for 7UP were intensively focused:

- Increase brand awareness with bottlers, consumers, and the trade.
- Maximize bottler support.
- Generate additional displays and feature ads.
- Motivate consumers to seek 7UP displays at retail.
- Increase frequency of purchase by consumers.

PROGRAM/STRATEGY

In 1984 The Seven-Up Company held exclusive soft drink promotional rights to the blockbuster movie "Indiana Jones and the Temple of Doom." This event focused on the week of the movie's release in May.

With consumers, a national FSI dropped that same week carrying a 30¢ coupon and a game card depicting one of five characters from the movie. Everybody who took the card to the in-store displays was a winner of two 50¢ coupons plus an Indiana Jones miniposter. Cards with character matches won a variety of higher-level prizes. ROP, carton stuffers, and bottle/can hangers completed distribution of the game card.

The trade enjoyed a Hollywood themed kick-off meeting and dealer loaders that included Indiana Jones hats, personalized director's chairs, T-shirts, and "Raiders of the Lost Ark" videocassettes. Bottlers gave a competitive price to the trade.

Bottlers learned about the promotion with film clips, promotional banners, route sales pocket reminder guides, and exciting premiums for sales personnel. The Seven-Up Company funded more than half of the costs for coupons and point of purchase, and all costs for the game prizes.

RESULTS

More than 90 percent of 7UP bottlers participated in this event, an all-time record. Nearly 600,000 entries arrived for the second chance drawing for unclaimed prizes and coupons redeemed 42 percent higher than the industry norm. June 1984 case sales increased 9.4 percent over those of the previous month.

The trade, bottlers, and consumers were clearly responsive to this blockbuster event.

1984-85

CAMPAIGN/EVENT

We Won't Go Back Without You

COMPANY

Coresco, Inc.

BRAND

Conrail Railways

YEAR/AWARD

1984-85/Silver

BACKGROUND/MARKETING SITUATION

Conrail provides piggyback rail service for freight movement. Railways were competing on a stiff basis to capture the freight movement from East to West. While Conrail experienced successful service into the Baltimore area, they had many empty trains heading back West.

OBJECTIVE

- Conrail had one key objective…to establish a user management profile which would aid in determining how Conrail could generate more actively in piggyback services to the West Coast.

PROGRAM/STRATEGY

In order to obtain the information needed, Conrail prepared an intrusive direct mail piece to force readership and completion of the questionnaire.

To separate the mailing piece from the many others routinely received, Conrail used a box and included a premium which quickly obtained the interest and curiosity of the recipient. The premium was a large wooden whistle with a sound that exactly replicated a train whistle. The copy on the printed materials related the premium to the problem at hand and quickly explained the information required, calling upon the recipient's "expertise" with the questionnaire.

RESULTS

Conrail received a 35 percent response to the questionnaire within two weeks of the mailing. With the help of a telemarketing campaign, Conrail achieved a whopping 85 percent response providing sufficient information through the questionnaire to address the issue of what was necessary to increase service to the West Coast.

1985-1986

REGGIE

AWARDS

CAMPAIGNS

"Where's the Cap'n?" Sweepstakes — The Quaker Oats Company

Spic and Span Diamond Jubilee — Procter & Gamble Company*

Contac Colds/Flu Alert — Menley & James

The Great Potato Chip Giveaway — Frito-Lay, Inc.

Castrol Money Back 12-Pack — Burmah-Castrol, Inc.

Search for Values — Del Monte Corporation

Five Weeks Shaving Absolutely Free — Wilkinson Sword Company

Create a Character Contest — Mattel Toys

Black & Decker Spacemaker Super Giveaway —
Black & Decker and Procter & Gamble Company*

Tax Time Relief Sweepstakes — Miles Laboratories, Inc./H & R Block

*Publication of the Procter & Gamble case study is restricted by company policy.

1985-86

CAMPAIGN/EVENT

"Where's the Cap'n?" Sweepstakes

COMPANY

Quaker Oats Company

BRAND

Cap'n Crunch cereal

YEAR/AWARD

1985-86/Gold/Super Reggie

BACKGROUND/MARKETING SITUATION

Cap'n Crunch cereal was the number two children's pre-sweetened cereal in the cereal industry, competing against more than a hundred brands in its category. The industry is also very large — more than 4 billion pounds of cereal are sold annually.

The Cap'n Crunch franchise had declined during 1985. It was perceived as old-fashioned and was struggling against newer licensed brands with unique, modern images. Pirates and sailing ships were not as attractive as newer characters like Pac Man, E.T., and the Smurfs.

OBJECTIVES

Several specific objectives were identified:
- Renew the Cap'n Crunch franchise.
- Generate trial among children 6 to 12.
- Make a dramatic package change.
- Encourage multiple purchase in order to achieve payout.
- Extend the reach of the promotion beyond the immediate target group if possible.

PROGRAM/STRATEGY

Quaker developed the theme "The Cap'n is missing. Where did he go?" to capture kids' imaginations and to rebuild sales. The following were components:
- The picture of the Cap'n was replaced with a "?" to illustrate the mystery graphically.
- A "3 in 1" Detective Kit was developed as an in-pack premium that kids could use to find the Cap'n.
- Three different packages, each with different clues for use in the Detective Kit, were developed.
- The promotion was supported with two separate FSI coupon/ads, Sunday comics, TV advertising, and a public relations campaign.
- Promotions to the trade included deals to generate displays and unique "talking" point of purchase materials.
- A separate college sweepstakes promotion using radio, different point-of–sale materials, and a rock video was developed.
- A separate Clean-up/Thank You sweepstakes to encourage purchase of residual package inventories was developed.

RESULTS

Cap'n Crunch did indeed renew the franchise! Shipments to the trade reached an all-time high during the month of October, and market share rose by 50 percent. Enthusiastic coverage in newspaper, on radio, and in magazine articles revealed the extent of national interest in solving the mystery of the Cap'n's whereabouts. Coverage included pieces in *USA Today*, "Saturday Night Live," and USA Cable Network. The rock video aired on MTV.

Perhaps most telling here is the evidence that the common wisdom of "product life cycle" may not be necessarily true. A carefully crafted restage can bring new meaning to the words "second chance."

1985-86

CAMPAIGN/EVENT
Contac Colds/Flu Alert

COMPANY
Menley & James, subsidiary of SmithKline Beecham

BRAND
Contac

YEAR/AWARD
1985-86/Gold

BACKGROUND/MARKETING SITUATION

In the early 1980s, the Federal Drug Administration changed its regulatory policy regarding prescription drugs. Many previously "controlled" drugs were moved to over-the-counter status and became readily available without a doctor's prescription. While this change seemed to benefit the general public, it meant more intense competition for the established brands in the cold products category.

In fact, by the mid-1980s, established brands such as Contac, Dristan, and Nyquil were struggling just to hold market share in the face of competition from new brands such as Sudafed, Actifed, and Drixoral. The battle for market share in this $400 million market was being fought at the point of sale. As brands battled for shelf space, advertising increased and consumer promotion spending quadrupled.

OBJECTIVES

For Menley & James, the objectives were clear.

CONSUMER
- Maintain Contac brand share in the face of increased competition and spending.
- Give current users an incentive to repurchase.
- Stimulate consumer trial among capsule users, one of the fastest growing segments in the cold products category.

TRADE

- Stimulate trade stockup.
- Stimulate trade promotion via ad features.
- Stimulate retail display, especially off-shelf secondary display presence, through increased trade involvement and promotion.

PROGRAM/STRATEGY

Menley & James developed a consumer promotion, the Contac Colds/Flu Alert, that reaffirmed the brand's leadership and positioned the brand as the authority on colds and flu. The promotion, which included consumer and trade programs, alerted consumers to colds and flu activity across the nation.

CONSUMER

- Televised flu alert announcements on NBC's "Today" with spokesperson Willard Scott and on ABC's "Good Morning America" for two seasons increased consumer awareness.
- Menley & James offered consumers added value at the retail level during the same two-season period with:
—A Colds/Flu Escape Hawaii Sweepstakes for 1984–85: 33 trips to Hawaii were featured on packages of Contac.
—A "Colds/Flu Protection Guide" for the 1985–86 season offered free at retail with a Contac purchase. All offers were flagged on the package.
- Consumer price incentives throughout the two seasons included national coupon events and instant coupons or refund offers.

TRADE

- Increased performance allowances and attractive terms were offered to stimulate stockup and local ads.
- Three deals per season were designed to facilitate stockup and local promotion.
- Menley & James ran a Contact Colds/Flu Alert sweepstakes for the trade.

RESULTS

CONSUMER

- Nielsen share objectives were achieved.
- Consumer involvement objectives, as measured by on-pack entries to the sweepstakes, exceeded forecast by 25 percent. Menley & James attributed this success to the synergistic effect of promotional TV support.
- Consumer coupon and refund redemptions exceeded previous levels by 25 percent.

TRADE

- Sales of Contac surpassed goals for the two-season period.
- Each season, 25,000 secondary displays were purchased and placed — 20 percent over the goal.
- Objectives for number and quality of Contac ads and features placed by the trade were achieved for both seasons.
- Special promotions by key customers in key regions quadrupled.

1985-86

CAMPAIGN/EVENT

The Great Potato Chip Picnic Giveaway

COMPANY

Frito-Lay, Inc.

BRANDS

Lays, Ruffles, O'Grady's

YEAR/AWARD

1985-86/Gold

BACKGROUND/MARKETING SITUATION

Frito-Lay marketed the only national line of flex bag potato chips. As the overall market leader in the potato chips category with three brands (Lays, Ruffles, and O'Grady's) and over 30 line items (various flavors and sizes), Frito-Lay potato chips faced aggressive regional competitive activity.

Mid-May through Labor Day is the peak season for potato chips. As brands strive for increased display and feature pricing, the consumer is confronted by numerous purchase incentives that erode brand loyalty. In this promotional clutter, Frito-Lay had two new chips to market: Ruffles Sour Cream and Cheddar and O'Grady's Hearty Seasonings, line extensions introduced in spring 1985 and needing a summer-long promotional event to sustain their momentum.

OBJECTIVES

Combining product introductions with the heaviest promotional push of the year was a challenge not to be taken lightly. Simply identifying objectives was daunting.

CONSUMER

- Increase sales during the key summer period.
- Generate and maintain consumer loyalty.
- Generate cross-brand trial, particularly among flavored items.
- Encourage "trade-up" to larger sizes.

TRADE

- Maintain continuous in-store promotional support in primary locations.
- Generate full-line merchandising support for all promoted brands.
- Gain key-week (Memorial Day and Fourth of July) feature display and support.

PROGRAM/STRATEGY

Frito-Lay knew that fielding a joint potato chip event would build cost efficiencies and a united front against the flood of regional activity. Thus, the plan aimed to collectively leverage the strengths and franchises of each of the three brands by using a simple, consistent theme.

This theme was a trivia game, The Great Potato Chip Picnic Giveaway Game. Consumers who called 1-800-PICNICS were challenged by "The Picnic Expert" to answer three picnic-related trivia questions. Callers who answered the three questions correctly were awarded a coupon for a complimentary bag of potato chips and were automatically entered into a Grand Prize drawing for 10 trips for two to Hawaii. The game was announced on all bags; questions and answers rotated across the entire line to encourage cross-trial among the line. More questions and answers (nine) were found on larger bags, fewer (three) on smaller bags. Sample questions were given on point-of-sale tear pads. The phone game allowed direct interaction with the consumer and increased the sense of fun, excitement, and immediate reward.

To encourage summer-long displays, the trade was offered two picnic-related items: (1) an attractive Ingrid Picnic Sack for display during the first four weeks and (2) a $30 in-store drawing that offered $25 for cash or groceries and $5 in free coupons for Frito-Lay potato chips. The in-store drawing was scheduled for key-week ad support periods and during periods of high store traffic. These incentives were incremental to regional allowances for ad features and displays.

RESULTS

The Great Potato Chip Picnic Giveaway exceeded every objective:
- Display and feature support during key holiday weeks for Ruffles and Lays experienced a double-digit increase over 1984 activity.
- The trivia contest (over nine weekends) resulted in millions of phone calls and incidentally resolved a burning corporate debate as to whether or not consumers really did read Frito-Lay packages.

1985-86

CAMPAIGN/EVENT

Castrol Money Back 12-Pack

COMPANY

Burmah-Castrol, Inc.

BRAND

Castrol GTX motor oil

YEAR/AWARD

1985-86/Gold

BACKGROUND/MARKETING SITUATION

Castrol, the manufacturer of Castrol GTX motor oils, was America's fastest-growing premium multigrade engine lubricant in the mid-1980s. Castrol GTX was positioned in the market as the motor oil engineered for smaller cars. Its market share in the Do-It-Yourself (DYI) market was up to 85 percent since 1981, although the category as a whole remained flat.

But 12 motor oil brands fighting for limited shelf space in a no-growth market meant retailers could manipulate motor oil as a "loss leader" to increase store traffic. By pitting brand against brand, retailers created motor oil price wars and exacerbated declining retail price points.

As the premium motor oil in the marketplace, Castrol was especially concerned that consumer rebates were eroding its price points. Competitors relied heavily on rebates, but such activity worked against Castrol's distinctive premium image and hurt profit margins.

OBJECTIVE

The company began to look for an alternative promotional concept that would encourage consumer trial and generate trade enthusiasm without lower prices. This concept would have to reward loyal users in a unique manner and, at the same time, encourage retailers to offer more frequent, bigger on-sale ads.

PROGRAM/STRATEGY

Castrol developed the Castrol Money Back 12-Pack, a promotion that provided the consumer an "added-value" bonus with each purchase. The promotion centered on a rebate booklet containing 16 famous name car care product rebates together worth $45. Products included Prestone Antifreeze,

Castrol
Money Back
12-Pack
$45.⁰⁰ Rebate Book
in every 12-Pack
on these quality
car care products.

Prestone Superflush, STP Gas Treatment, STP Son of a Gun Protectant, Simonize Car Wax, Purolator Filters, Espree Wheel Car Products, ND Spark Plugs, Black & Decker Tire Inflator and Car Scrubber, Bondo Body Repair Supplies, GoJo Hand Cleaners, and Castrol's Automatic Transmission Fluid and Brake Fluid. The booklet also included a half-price subscription to *Road and Track* magazine plus a self-liquidating Castrol apparel offer. However, the booklet did *not* offer a rebate on Castrol GTX.

The program was promoted direct to the consumer as well as through the trade. Spot TV aimed at men 18 to 49 was run on all three major networks. Spot radio was used in key Castrol markets. A special Money Back 12-Pack commercial tag was offered to retailers. In-store promotion included easel-back posters, free-hanging posters, shelf-talkers, case cards, and a cross-merchandising shelf-talker. In addition, the booklet was placed in every Castrol GTX and Heavy Duty 12 one-quart cases during the August 3–November 4, 1985 period (October is National Car Care Month).

RESULTS

By the end of the promotional period, Castrol's total gallon volume sales were up 18.3% in a no-growth category. In addition, and perhaps more important, the Money Back 12-Pack gave the company 14 months of rebate-free growth. The promotion was an unqualified success because it increased sales, increased store traffic, and rewarded loyal customers, while leaving the on-sale price point unscathed.

1985-86

CAMPAIGN/EVENT
Search for Values

COMPANY
Del Monte Corporation

BRANDS
Multiple brands

YEAR/AWARD
1985-86/Silver

BACKGROUND/MARKETING SITUATION

The Del Monte Corporation had a full line of food products competing in discrete markets. To counter their varied competition, Del Monte sought a storewide umbrella promotion suitable to the needs and satisfaction of its sales force, the trade, and consumers.

OBJECTIVES

The goals were to increase consumer awareness of Del Monte product diversity and to stimulate trade involvement, especially favorable product features and pricing.

PROGRAM/STRATEGY

The Search for Values sweepstakes was developed as the "call for action" that would accomplish Del Monte's goal.

Del Monte announced the consumer portion through ROP (56MM circ.), ethnic print (3MM), and in-store sweepstakes pads. The offer was structured to enhance a "base prize" when the consumer demonstrated a commitment to finding additional Del Monte feature ads. Each entry had to include

Del Monte ads (originals, no copies) from retail grocers' ads to qualify. Sweepstakes winners were awarded a prize dependent on the number of ads attached to their entry form (limit 10 different ads). Thus, a qualified first prize winner was assured a $2,500 cash prize. If that winner included five feature ads, the prize multiplied five times to $12,500. If that winner included 10 ads, the prize was increased to $25,000.

To increase store traffic and to ensure trade participation, numerous store-redeemed coupon offers were also distributed.

RESULTS

Corporate goals for the promotion were met. Specific results are considered proprietary and could not be released in this publication. The sweepstakes generated more than a million entries, about three times the industry norm.

1985-86

CAMPAIGN/EVENT
Five Weeks Shaving Absolutely Free

COMPANY
Wilkinson Sword Company

AGENCY
American Marketing Services, Inc.

YEAR/AWARD
1985-86/Silver

BACKGROUND/MARKETING SITUATION

As the result of a technical innovation, Wilkinson wanted to introduce a new "retractable" disposable razor into the market in 1985. The company, long known as a manufacturer of fine cutting knives, had tried to enter the shaving market 10 years earlier. That first product had limited success and was withdrawn.

Research indicated that the new Wilkinson razor was superior to Bic Disposable Razors and at parity with Gillette Disposable Razors, the chief competition in the market. The challenge was to identify Bic and Gillette users by type and to use a variety of trial techniques to influence purchase of the Wilkinson product. With limited funds, the company had to penetrate the market, generate trial, and create a franchise.

OBJECTIVES

A combination of consumer and trade objectives was identified:

CONSUMER
- Create selected trial targeted against Gillette and Bic users.
- Create a minimum trial incentive against Bic users and a maximum incentive against Gillette users.

TRADE
- Obtain distribution plus feature and display activity.

PROGRAM/STRATEGY

A free-standing insert with the quip "Bet Ya 2 Weeks of Free Shaving You'll Quit" was designed to include a self-mailer shipping container. Consumers were invited to send Wilkinson their current disposable razors in the self-mailers.

A variety of trial offers was returned to participants, depending on their current brand. Bic users received five 20-cent coupons good for Wilkinson disposable razors. Gillette users received a coupon for a free five-pack of Wilkinson disposable razors and one free Wilkinson disposable razor.

The trade received a similar offer, with a changed headline: "Bet $5.40 a Case Your Customers Will Switch."

RESULTS

This time around Wilkinson Sword scored a victory.

On the consumer level, in the first week following the FSI, more than 10 percent of the circulation of the FSI was received. The eventual total redemption rate exceeded 20 percent of circulation, although only 50 percent of households use disposable razors.

In the trade, markets that received the FSI distribution exceeded the objective by more than 25 percent.

As another indication of the phenomenal success of the program was that news articles on the program appeared in *Advertising Age* and *The New York Times.*

1985-86

CAMPAIGN/EVENT
Create a Character Contest

COMPANY
Mattel Toys

BRAND
Masters of the Universe

AGENCY
Don Jagoda Associates

YEAR/AWARD
1985-86/Silver

BACKGROUND/MARKETING SITUATION

Mattel Toys had a long, successful history dating back to the introduction of the Barbie doll in 1958. By 1985, it maintained a balanced mix of classic toys like Barbie and new, preemptive toys including the Masters of the Universe.

The Masters of the Universe product line competed aggressively in the volatile male action figures category. It had consistently led its category, and Mattel was determined to keep it in that position in the face of increased competition during the year.

OBJECTIVES

Mattel had four objectives to address:
- Maximize brand awareness.
- Increase sales and multiple
  purchases.
- Develop a selling tool for the sales force that would incorporate a local retailing option.
- Create publicity to support a significant existing TV campaign.

PROGRAM/STRATEGY

Mattel realized there was the potential for establishing a new level of loyalty among consumers and the trade if an event could be conceived that would be fun for children while it earned the respect of their parents, too. The Create a Character Contest was therefore planned to reward the children's creativity by asking them to design a new action figure for Masters of the Universe, with the winning figure actually being made into a toy.

The promotion included an entry and judging period followed by a national vote for the ultimate figure, but it was planned that each child who entered would win recognition and a gift. The contest was launched with a press conference and all details for entry printed in the Sunday Comics in September. To enter, each child had to draw a new figure, provide a name, explain its unique characteristics, and then submit the entry with two Masters proofs-of-purchase, or simply name three different Masters characters on a separate piece of paper. All entrants received a Masters comic book and character magnets.

Three months later, from tens of thousands of entrants judged based on previously determined criteria, five finalists were featured in the Sunday comics. Kids could vote for their favorite by calling a 900 phone number. More than a thousand prizes, with total value around $300,000, went to semifinalists and finalists. Prizes included scholarships and

Masters of the Universe toy collections. The grand prize winner also received a trip to Los Angeles with the right to be honorary President of Mattel for a day.

The trade supported the promotion with in-store point-of-sale displays with free Masters of the Universe posters and entry forms.

RESULTS

The grand prize winner gleaned 30 percent of the more than 140,000 calls received in less than a week. The sell-through of Masters of the Universe figures more than doubled versus the previous selling period. National publicity was received for all phases of the program. The contest winner received press coverage in national publications including *Newsweek, USA Today,* and toy trade publications. Even "Good Morning, America" picked up the story. Because Mattel recognized that child's play is serious business, the company reaped rich rewards for the efforts expended.

1985-86

CAMPAIGN/EVENT

Tax Time Relief Sweepstakes

COMPANY

Miles Laboratories, Inc. Consumer Healthcare Division/H&R Block

BRAND

Alka-Seltzer; Tax Preparation Services

YEAR/AWARD

1985-86/Silver

BACKGROUND/MARKETING SITUATION

For years, Alka-Seltzer has been a leading over-the-counter (OTC) antacid/analgesic. It has nearly universal distribution and consumer awareness, yet it faces a constant flood of new products, so it needs to be viewed as modern and timely. Alka-Seltzer competes tenaciously for limited floor display space because sales increase as much as 400 percent from such displays. Like Alka-Seltzer, H&R Block enjoys national recognition, but its business is strictly seasonal in consumer minds.

OBJECTIVES

Primary objectives were:
- Sell-in 50 percent more Alka-Seltzer floor displays.
- Ensure that incremental numbers of displays were actually installed.
- Move incremental volumes of Alka-Seltzer.
- Increase traffic in H&R Block offices.

PROGRAM/STRATEGY

Tax time is a major source of symptoms of headache and upset stomach. A tie-in promotion that would offer the consumer two kinds of relief—relief from the symptoms of stress and relief from financial worry—would capture the imagination of consumers and increase traffic and revenue for both Alka-Seltzer and H&R Block.

The program had two phases: consumer and trade. The consumer promotion included a Tax Time Relief Sweepstakes with a grand prize of a lifetime of free tax services from H&R Block, plus a trip to the Bahamas and $5,000 in cash. A bonus of $5,000 was awarded to the grand prize winner if the entry was validated in an H&R Block office. A :30 commercial featuring Alka-Seltzer and H&R Block ran on network television during the promotional period. Point-of-purchase materials included easel cards set up in H&R Block offices and near-packed free tax tips given away with purchase of Alka-Seltzer from in-store displays. A national FSI announcing the sweepstakes and providing a coupon good for Alka-Seltzer also stirred response.

The trade promotion included floor displays with the Tax Time Relief Sweepstakes entry form on a header card, shelf-talkers with the sweepstakes entry, and a $5,000 donation to charity in the name of the store from which the winning entry was picked. In addition, the sales force got the chance to win free tax service for one year.

RESULTS

For Alka-Seltzer, all objectives were achieved:
- Sixty percent increase in the number of displays sold.
- Eighty percent increase in ACV display in food stores.
- Five hundred percent increase in displays sold to drug stores.
- Significant increase in factory sales volume for the February–April period.
  For H&R Block, the results could not be released.

1986-1987

REGGIE

AWARDS

CAMPAIGNS

Case of the Missing Case — Miller Brewing Company

Apple Open House 1986 — Apple Computer, Inc.

Hot & Spicy Favorites — Miles Laboratories, Inc.

Countdown to Christmas — The Seven-Up Company

Go For It America! Sweepstakes — British Airways

Armor All Instant-Win Game — McKesson Corporation

Grand Jeu Elf/Antar Scratch-And-Win Game — Elf France Petroleum Company

Sheraton Presents Monday Night Madness — ITT Sheraton Hotel Corporation

Pepsi Cola Popbox — Pepsi Cola Group

The Dr Pepper Call To Action — Dr Pepper/Seven-Up Companies, Inc.

1986-87

CAMPAIGN/EVENT

The Case of the Missing Case

COMPANY

Miller Brewing Company

BRAND

Miller Lite

YEAR/AWARD

1986-87/Gold/Super Reggie

BACKGROUND/MARKETING SITUATION

In 1986, Miller Lite was second in beer sales in the nation, outselling all other light beers. Beer consumption is highest around holidays, and Memorial Day is a high-volume consumption period.

Each Memorial Day, Miller Lite was again "immortalized" by "The Lite All-Star Alumni" TV commercial in which former pro athletes met at an annual reunion. This humorous spot, a blend of advertising and promotion, aimed at achieving critical support from consumers and retailers, because, unlike other packaged goods producers, the beer industry is forbidden by law to pay fees for feature ads and display space. Promotions that drive consumers into stores to find their favorite beer displays figure heavily in trade decisions to devote floor and ad space to particular brands. Consequently, one way to gauge a promotion's success is to count feature ads and displays relative to those of competitors.

OBJECTIVES

A tenth reunion spot featuring the All-Stars was imminent and it would have to meet these objectives:

- Secure feature ads and display by demonstrating promotional commitment through media placements in conjunction with sell-in to the trade.
- Encourage consumers to trade up from six and twelve packs to case packs.

PROGRAM/STRATEGY

The basic strategy envisioned an intriguing event that could be extended into radio promotion and public relations. Using the theme The Case of the Missing Case enabled Miller to ask consumers to solve the mystery of who stole the case of Miller Lite from the reunion bash. Amateur sleuths got clues on TV and at point-of-sale. Studying clues and guessing the answer made consumers eligible to win one of more than $100,000 in prizes.

CONSUMER
- A $100,000 sweepstakes to entice consumers to determine the culprit.
- A series of "Who Dunnit" and "Clue" commercials during March and April capitalized on the national mystery craze.
- Encouraging consumers through TV, print, and radio advertising to solve the crime in-store.
- Additional clues on game cards.
- Creating urgency to solve the crime by announcing a solution commercial on June 1.
- Advertising in *T.V. Guide* and Sunday papers announced the scheduled debut of a solution commercial.
- Extending the campaign with "Case Chase" radio promotions.

TRADE
- Price-offs (where legal) on Miller Lite.
- Overlay refunds in select underdeveloped markets.
- Trade advertising placement to coincide with the March–April sell-in period.
- Staging initial "Who Dunnit" and "Clue" spots in March and April to motivate retail participation through May.
- Sales film complete with a series of Case of the Missing Case commercials and promotional spots.
- Display materials based on the promotional theme.
- Disclosing print media buy to stimulate trade.
- Slicks for trade feature activity.

RESULTS

Memorial Day feature ad activity for Miller Lite reached an all-time high, and during May Miller recorded its largest sales month in the history of the brand. The public relations campaign generated more than 26 million impressions, further evidence of consumer enthusiasm for the promotion.

1986-87

CAMPAIGN/EVENT

Apple Open House 1986

COMPANY

Apple Computer, Inc.

BRAND

Apple IIGS

AGENCY

U.S. Communications Corporation

YEAR/AWARD

1986-87/Gold

BACKGROUND/MARKETING SITUATION

Since 1977, Apple Computer had manufactured hardware and software for home, business, and education applications. Apple had always been an innovative, aggressive force in the microcomputer industry. In the mid-1980s, the company ranked number one in the educational computer market and number two overall in the personal computer industry.

In 1986, Apple faced two key promotional issues. For Apple, as for the entire personal computer industry, the year-end holiday was a critical selling time. More than 50 percent of annual sales occur during this period. Apple, like its competitors, needed category excitement generated prior to the peak buying season. In addition, Apple was not only competing against other computer brands, but also against big-ticket, high-technology consumer purchases like VCRs, camcorders, and videodisc players. Nonetheless, it appeared that Apple's competitors would not be helping to heat up sales with their own promotional events.

Announcing the Apple Open House.

Coming soon to a mall near you.

Apple's market research continued to confirm the traditional barriers to consumer purchases of computers: fear of technology, lack of perceived benefits, and misconceptions about affordability.

OBJECTIVES

Apple needed a dynamic, break-through promotional event to stimulate consumer interest and to communicate the benefits of its product line. Also, in September 1986 Apple introduced an exciting new product, the Apple IIGS (acronym for Graphics and Sound). Apple sought an opportunity to demonstrate this new product.

Specific objectives included:
- Generate primary consumer demand prior to the approaching holiday selling season.
- Encourage consumer hands-on introduction to Apple products, especially the new Apple IIGS.
- At the sales force and dealer levels, renew excitement about and confidence in the consumer home computer market.

PROGRAM/STRATEGY

Apple brought its products into the friendly, high-traffic environment of shopping malls. The "Apple Open House" became the first traveling mall show in the computer industry. It premiered in 26 malls in key markets across the country between September 26 and November 16.

The following approaches were used to create a high-impact presence:
- Valuable premiums ($3–$5 value) for anyone who tried an Apple Computer: children, teens, and adults all received a "demo chit" to redeem for their free gift.
- A sweepstakes awarding a limited edition Apple IIGS to the winner and five Apple IIe's for the school of the winner's choice. This sweepstakes ran in all 26 markets.
- Free "Apple Open House" shopping bags for all visitors.
- In-mall displays to reinforce Apple's image and to create a homey environment.
- A variety of easily understood demonstrations explaining what an Apple computer could do for a family.
- A professional 15-minute live stage presentation featuring the new Apple IIGS programs.
- Brochures answering consumer questions about Apple computers.
- Friendly sales staff who wore special Open House uniforms and buttons that said, "Ask me about your free gift."
- Local listing of dealers and Apple user groups on a market-by-market basis.

RESULTS

Mall traffic was estimated at a minimum of 10,000 per site, resulting in over 250,000 impressions. Apple handed out around 4,000 premiums per mall. There were over 100,000 valid consumer entries for the sweepstakes.

Local public relations liked the story and generated interest well into the following year. Despite extra weekend work, the sales force was extremely enthusiastic about the event because it provided them an opportunity to learn the issues and concerns of the consumer. Both sales reps and dealers asked for a repeat of the event. Also, and most important, Apple exceeded its 1986 holiday sales projections.

1986-87

CAMPAIGN/EVENT

Hot & Spicy Favorites

COMPANY

Miles Laboratories, Inc., Consumer Healthcare Division

BRAND

Alka-Seltzer

YEAR/AWARD

1986-87/Gold

BACKGROUND/MARKETING SITUATION

Alka-Seltzer was a leading over-the-counter (OTC) antacid/analgesic with almost universal distribution and consumer awareness. It could relieve symptoms of nausea and headache associated with overindulgence in hot and spicy food.

The OTC analgesic market focuses efforts on getting additional floor display because displays generate significant incremental product movement. The logical tie-in partner for Alka-Seltzer would be any spicy food, but that possibility was understandably remote. So how could displays be leveraged? The challenge was to encourage spicy food consumption among consumers and to generate significant trade support.

OBJECTIVES

The following were promotion objectives:
- Increase factory shipments by 15 percent.
- Increase the number of displays installed by 5 percent.
- Reinforce the "Alka-Seltzer to the Rescue" ad campaign using the "Chili" :30 commercial.
- Provide consumers with an incentive for repeat purchase.

PROGRAM/STRATEGY

The promotion had two facets: a consumer-oriented program and a trade-directed program.

NEAR PACK COOKBOOK

FREE STANDING INSERT

SHELF TALKER/TEAR OFF PAD

CONSUMER

Miles offered a free recipe booklet via Alka-Seltzer near-packs. It contained recipes from Better Homes and Gardens for hot and spicy chili, Mexican, Cajun, and barbecued foods. The booklet was free with the purchase of Alka-Seltzer from a floor display or mail-in offer. In addition, the booklet contained discount coupons for Alka-Seltzer, spicy food ingredients, and an offer for other Better Homes and Gardens cookbooks at 50 percent off their regular price. A national FSI and tear-off pads publicized the offer. A total of 775,000 booklets was produced for the promotion.

TRADE

The Alka-Seltzer pre-pack display was designed to resemble a kitchen range with a spice rack. Store management and buyers were mailed a promotional tube that included a copy of Better Homes & Gardens' "Hot & Spicy Favorites," an "Alka-Seltzer to the Rescue" bib, and a chili spoon with a hole burned through it.

RESULTS

The following were the results of this most successful program:
- Display shipments were up 20 percent above the seasonal norm.
- A total of 10,000 displays were placed nationwide.
- In-store displays in food stores increased more than 20 percent and in drug stores more than 100 percent.
- Special feature pricing increased 7 percent in food stores and 43 percent in drug stores.
- The "Hot & Spicy Favorites" recipe booklet was picked up on "Late Night with David Letterman" as a novel consumer offer.

1986-87

CAMPAIGN/EVENT
Countdown to Christmas

COMPANY
The Seven-Up Company

BRAND
7UP

YEAR/AWARD
1986-87/Gold

BACKGROUND/MARKETING SITUATION

In the mid-1980s, 7UP was the number one lemon-lime soft drink in the world, with a 53 percent share of the domestic lemon-lime segment. All brands in the soft drink industry were consistently parity priced and had universal availability. A major disadvantage for 7UP was its limited amount of available display space, which was far less than that of the "cola giants," Coke and Pepsi. In addition, the holiday season, which traditionally belonged to 7UP, had come under attack by Slice and Sprite.

OBJECTIVES

The 1986 holiday push meant a chance to re-establish 7UP as the premier holiday lemon-lime soft drink. Related objectives were:
- Maximize volume through display.
- Give 7UP a point of difference—provide value beyond price.

PROGRAM/STRATEGY

The strategy was to develop a totally integrated holiday marketing program that clearly positioned 7UP as the premier drink in its market. The primary strategy was the development of the Countdown to Christmas near-pack poster premium that gave value beyond price to accelerate purchase volume and gave retailers a compelling reason for display.

The program included:
- Posters of the 7UP Gnomes, modified versions of Santa's elves. They became the creative icons for a holiday poster near-pack that delivered 7UP's holiday message, "7UP...the Feeling of Christmas."
- Promotional :30 TV commercials to support the near-pack poster offer delivered during nine animated Christmas specials.
- A national FSI supporting the in-store poster offer, plus a 25¢ off coupon.
- Trade advertising to introduce and pre-sell the free poster offer.
- Full array of 7UP Gnome-themed point-of-purchase materials.
- Corrugated Santa's Workshop Playhouse that served triple duty as a trade loader, a display piece, and an in-store prize.
- A national public relations event, The 7UP Gnome Tour '86, which extended the poster offer into a nationwide event (32 children's hospitals in 24 cities beginning December 1 and concluding on Christmas Eve).
- A variety of in-store sweepstakes items, all utilizing the Gnomes.
- Gnomes helping local bottlers to host parties at participating hospitals.
- Bottlers donating $5,000 to each hospital.

RESULTS

Results of the program were as follows:
- Bottler participation was the highest ever for any 7UP promotion. Seventy-five percent of 7UP bottlers, representing 85 percent of the volume, executed the poster program, with over 3 million posters distributed.
- The TV promotional spot generated more than 200 direct telephone requests for the poster.
- Many retailers who usually did not display 7UP called for the poster to satisfy requests from their customers.
- Sales volume for December was the highest of any month of the year.
- The Gnome Tour reached an audience of 23 million and earned over $125,000 in donations to children's hospitals.

1986-87

CAMPAIGN/EVENT

"Go For It, America!" Sweepstakes

COMPANY

British Airways

AGENCY

The Howard Marlboro Group

YEAR/AWARD

1986-87/Gold

BACKGROUND/MARKETING SITUATION

British Airways was the world's largest and most profitable international airline. In 1986, it carried more than 16 million passengers to 143 cities in 68 countries on six continents. Reservations had declined severely early in the year due to fear surrounding terrorist activity and related military activity. There was a net loss of 27,000 bookings alone during the week following the April 14 air raid by the United States on Libya. Competitors were suffering similar losses.

OBJECTIVES

British Airways had to assure American travelers that the advantages of air travel to Europe outweighed their fears of terrorist reprisals. Thus, the objectives of the promotion were to:

- Increase passengers on the British Airways North American route.
- Increase awareness that British Airways flies to England and other European destinations from 20 gateway cities in the United States.

PROGRAM/STRATEGY

The consumer strategy and trade strategy each addressed both objectives.

CONSUMER

A kick-off announcement on June 10 in morning and evening papers boasted a sweepstakes for 5,200 free seats on all British Airways flights from the United States to London. Monthly continuity programs offered passengers luxury prizes for playing two games.
- An in-flight skill game ($750 value) guaranteed one passenger would be a winner on each flight to London.
- A scratch-off instant-win game offered a chance to win a major prize worth $100,000 (e.g., a ride on the Concorde, a shopping spree at Harrod's, a Rolls-Royce) to pre-boarding passengers. All prizes were British themed.

TRADE

A kick-off package containing bumper stickers, buttons, T-shirts, window banners, and counter cards was mailed to major travel agents. Every month, 30,000 travel agents received themed promotional materials that corresponded to media ads.

Supporting the trade and consumer programs, British Airways developed heavy public relations activity for the June 10 kickoff event. A press conference in New York and special events in London, including tea with Margaret Thatcher for a few of the winners, were also held.

RESULTS

One million entries were received in the first week of the sweepstakes. Net bookings increased to 64,000 a week, compared to the loss of 27,000 during the week following the raid on Libya. Within 60 days, British Airways' load factor had returned to that of the previous year, reflecting the dramatic turnaround in the attitudes of Americans traveling abroad.

1986-87

CAMPAIGN/EVENT
Armor All Instant-Win Game

COMPANY
McKesson Corporation

BRANDS
Armor All automotive finish protectors

AGENCY
Joseph Potocki & Associates

YEAR/AWARD
1986-87/Silver

BACKGROUND/MARKETING SITUATION

Boasting a 90 percent brand share, Armor All dominated the protectant segment of the automotive appearance chemicals category. Its growth rate had averaged 20 percent per year. In 1986, there were 792 car wash operations participating in the Armor All service program.

Nearly 50 percent of the consuming public used car washes, so creating demand for the product at car washes was an important goal in expanding sales. Since nearly 70 percent of Armor All's sales were impulse, any good promotional effort that created consumer awareness would increase sales.

OBJECTIVE

When a company reaches 90 percent share, it needs to guard against complacency. Armor All was determined to protect its position and franchise.

CONSUMER
- Create awareness and trial.
- Increase frequency among current users.
- Maintain/enhance the Armor All image.

TRADE

- Gain new distribution— a target of 200 new car washes.
- Provide promotional support to these critical outlets.
- Provide an incentive for the trade to use merchandise programs.

PROGRAM/STRATEGY

A high-visibility promotion that would build consumer awareness and increased demand for the product was developed. The main components were:

- An instant-win game. All car wash customers received a rub-off game card that awarded a free Ford Mustang, a Sony FM stereo headset, free Armor All Tire Service, or a $1 coupon good on any Armor All service for everyone.
- The game (5 million cards) was supported by window posters, pump tents, and menu signs at the car wash.
- To encourage trade participation, a car wash employee incentive sweepstakes was linked to consumer game cards redeemed for the Armor All service.

RESULTS

The results of the promotion were:

- Of the 792 car washes already using Armor All, more than 470 outlets participated in the promotion.
- An additional 215 distributors (7.5 percent above target) signed for Armor All service as a result of the program.
- Bulk product sales increased $413,000 during the period (vs. prior year)—a 203 percent increase in dollar sales.
- Armor All profits increased 20 percent during the promotion.
  This company proved it could protect more than automobiles.

1986-87

CAMPAIGN/EVENT

Grand Jeu Elf/Antar Scratch-And-Win Game

COMPANY

Elf France Petroleum Company

BRANDS

Batteries, tires, and accessories

AGENCY

International Promotion Consultants (IPC/Paris)

YEAR/AWARD

1986-87/Silver

BACKGROUND/MARKETING SITUATION

Elf France was a major player in the gasoline, lubricants, batteries, tires, and accessories (BTA) category in France. Its products were marketed to consumers through gas stations (e.g., Shell, Exxon, and Elf) under either the ELF or ANTAR trademarks. In the mid-1980s, its shares of the gasoline and lubricants markets were over 20 percent.

The BTA category is primarily a parity market. The main consumer concerns are car care in preparation for long trips and selecting the best service station. Motorists were Elf's largest market, and the summer travel season was the primary buying and promotion time of the year.

OBJECTIVES

The objectives for the program were straightforward:
- Make the greatest number of motorists possible stop at Elf gas stations.
- Give consumers the chance to compare Elf products with its competitors.
- Increase repeat purchase.
- Surpass prior year sales.

PROGRAM/STRATEGY

Elf gave consumers the opportunity to play a free game of chance, a scratch-and-win game using tickets. The winning ticket was worth 20,000 French Francs (about $3,000 U.S.). Other ticket holders could win any of a range of prizes, from a box of candy to larger awards. Tickets were mailed to 6 million consumers, and an additional 35 million tickets were available through the network of 3,500 Elf dealers. Ads for the game were placed on TV and radio and in consumer magazines. Each winner had to come into an Elf station either to claim a lower level prize or to fill out a prize payment application for higher level prizes.

RESULTS

The following were the results of the program:

- More than 99 percent of winning game cards were redeemed.
- Sales of gasoline increased 5 percent.
- Market share for gasoline increased from 20.7 percent to 21.5 percent.
- Sales of lubricants increased 13 percent.
- Market share for lubricants increased from 20.2 percent to 21.7 percent.

1986-87

CAMPAIGN/EVENT

Sheraton Presents Monday Night Madness

COMPANY

Sheraton Hotel Corporation

BRAND

ITT Sheraton Hotel lounges

AGENCY

Focus Marketing, Inc.

YEAR/AWARD

1986-87/Silver

BACKGROUND/MARKETING SITUATION

Sheraton has long been a leader in the hotel industry. The Sheraton parent corporation wanted to increase the use of Sheraton lounges by both hotel guests and local residents. Sheraton also needed a promotion that would motivate guests to increase requests for room service, especially on Monday nights, one of the least profitable evenings of the week.

OBJECTIVES

The following were the program objectives:
- Increase room service food and beverage sales.
- Increase lounge food and beverage sales.
- Establish lounge patronage from the surrounding community.
- Establish continuity and repeat traffic on Monday nights.

PROGRAM/ STRATEGY

The program Sheraton Presents Monday Night Madness invited hotel guests and the community to "score big" in the lounge with a sweepstakes that was easy to play. The plan capitalized on the Monday Night Football phenomenon. Entry forms had to be dropped off on the game board in the lounge of the hotel. Winners were drawn at the end of each game. This was a compelling reason to visit the lounge and reminded guests to watch the game (as they ate dinner in their rooms or in the lounge). Prizes included a weekend getaway, a dinner for two, and a selection of low-level items. Everyone entering the local game was automatically entered into a national drawing to win Pro Bowl and Super Bowl tickets.

RESULTS

Room service and lounge sales increased more than 300 percent during the promotion period. In addition, Sheraton hotels gleaned ample positive publicity.

1986-87

CAMPAIGN/EVENT

Pepsi Cola Popbox

COMPANY

Pepsi Cola Group

BRANDS

Multiple Pepsi brands

AGENCY

American Consulting Corporation

YEAR/AWARD

1986-87/Silver

BACKGROUND/MARKETING SITUATION

Pepsi Cola routinely battles Coca-Cola for supremacy in the soft drink category. This struggle is intensified during the summer when consumption of soft drinks reaches its peak. During this period, consumers watch for price features and frequently switch brands to save money. The trade rotates features and displays between Pepsi and Coke.

In 1986, Pepsi felt locked into price promotions, because most other promotion vehicles required packaging changes and dual inventories, activities that were time consuming and expensive at the manufacturer level and resisted by many retailers as difficult to implement. Pepsi was determined to find a better way.

OBJECTIVES

Objectives for the promotion were to retain brand switchers in the Pepsi franchise throughout the peak summer consumption period and to inspire retailers to maintain Pepsi displays for four weeks.

PROGRAM/ STRATEGY

To support brand loyalty and repeat purchase, a two-level continuity program was developed. Consumers could collect specially marked proofs-of-purchase worth points toward their choice of several prizes. To receive $5 in Pepsi coupons, the consumer collected 275 points. To receive a choice of $10 in cash, a stereo headphone radio, a portable stereo radio, or a digital clock radio, the consumer collected 400 points.

To facilitate collecting and mailing the bottle caps and pull tabs used as proofs, Pepsi developed the "popbox," a self-mailing collection box printed with the program details and a tally grid to keep a running record of the number of proofs saved. The consumer merely wrote his or her name and address on the box, checked off the prize choice, taped the box, and mailed it. Flattened popboxes were shipped pre-packed to retailers, who then offered them free to consumers. Route sales representatives replenished the pre-packs as needed. Four weeks of radio and TV promotional spots urged consumers to get the popboxes at their stores and thus obliged retailers to maintain the displays.

RESULTS

It is usually difficult to measure the degree of success in a long-term continuity program. For this program, however, research was conducted in three phases. The names of consumers who took popboxes were collected in-store. Mid-program and program-end callbacks followed. It revealed that:

- Three-quarters of the original participants continued with the program.
- Participants increased their purchases on all participating Pepsi brands.
- Consumer sales increased from 10 to 60 percent across three different sizes.

Based on category consumption patterns for the time period, the proof structure not only required total commitment to Pepsi brands for a two-month period but also stretched consumption far beyond normal levels.

In fact, redemption of popboxes was twice the quantity projected in a pre-test. Pepsi had found the better way.

1986-87

CAMPAIGN/EVENT
The Dr Pepper Call to Action

COMPANY
Dr Pepper/Seven-Up Companies, Inc.

BRAND
Diet Dr Pepper

YEAR/AWARD
1986-87/Silver

BACKGROUND/MARKETING SITUATION

The diet soft drink segment had become increasingly competitive during the mid-1980s as the category increased in popularity with the public. Diet Dr Pepper was a distinctive soft drink, and research had shown that consumers felt it delivered the taste of regular Dr Pepper, although it had only two calories. Yet since 1983, Diet Dr Pepper had suffered serious market share erosion due to the introduction of major competitive brands. It was crucial that the company re-establish brand image, recover the brand's earlier momentum, and regain bottler support.

OBJECTIVES

The following were the primary objectives for Diet Dr Pepper:

- Create an event presence in the marketplace that would generate heavy trial and awareness among consumers by breaking through heavy competitive advertising.
- Achieve increased shelf space and more end-aisle displays.
- Regain bottler support for the brand.

PROGRAM/ STRATEGY

A two-pronged promotion to consumers and to bottlers was developed.

CONSUMER

To generate awareness and induce trial, Dr Pepper gave a

free can of Diet Dr Pepper to every consumer who called a toll-free number. The offer, The Dr Pepper Call to Action, was made in 250 markets in a :30 TV commercial featuring John Albers, the president of the company.

TRADE

The Call to Action sampling program got full support at the retailer and bottler level. Radio and TV spots, newspaper ads, displays, point-of-purchase graphics, on-pack coupons, feature trade support ads, and a full public relations campaign were all themed to the Call to Action.

RESULTS

Diet Dr Pepper sales for participating markets indexed 60 percent higher than those for nonparticipating markets. Consumer telephone response was approximately 1 percent, on-target based on previous test market forecasts. At the bottler level, 99 percent signed up for the program, and 80 percent of those ordered point-of-purchase, merchandiser, and sampling materials. Retail chains featured Call To Action single-can displays and heavy discounts to induce trial. Diet Dr Pepper had stemmed its erosion.

1987-1988

REGGIE

AWARDS

CAMPAIGNS

TOP GUN — PEPSI COLA COMPANY

MAXWELL HOUSE TASTE OF CHICAGO — GENERAL FOODS U.S.A.

MILLER/DRAGNET SWEEPSTAKES — MILLER BREWING COMPANY

WISK BRIGHT NIGHTS '87 — LEVER BROTHERS COMPANY

SHELTER AID — JOHNSON & JOHNSON CONSUMER PRODUCTS

THE NIKE CHALLENGE — NIKE, INC.

THE GREAT AMERICAN KEY HUNT — THE PROCTER & GAMBLE COMPANY AND
CHEVROLET MOTOR DIVISION, GENERAL MOTORS CORPORATION*

HARDEE'S CALIFORNIA RAISINS PROMOTION — HARDEE'S FOOD SYSTEMS, INC.

FREQUENT BUYER — FOOD WORLD, INC.

PLAY MONOPOLY AT MCDONALD'S — MCDONALD'S CORPORATION

1987-88

CAMPAIGN/EVENT
Pepsi Top Gun

COMPANY
Pepsi Cola Company

BRAND
Pepsi and Diet Pepsi

YEAR/AWARD
1987-88/Gold/Super Reggie

BACKGROUND/MARKETING SITUATION

Pepsi and Diet Pepsi were leading brands in the soft drink category in 1987. Pepsi was number one in food stores. Diet Pepsi was number two.

True to the "Cola Wars" legend, category awareness was driven by heavy media spending and ongoing promotion. Distribution was virtually universal with the grocery trade, but video stores were just emerging as opportunities for new distribution. To achieve solo distribution in a video store would be ideal.

OBJECTIVES

The objectives were to:
- Increase key food store retail display, total inventory, feature ads, and volume.
- Make similar increases in non-grocery and smaller stores.
- Provide bottlers with the tools and direction to develop new distribution in video stores.

PROGRAM/STRATEGY

The strategy was to tie-in with a product that would be highly visible in the video market and with the general public. The result was the Pepsi Top Gun promotion.

CONSUMER

- Diet Pepsi :60 Top Gun commercial placed in front of every "Top Gun" videocassette in video stores. This was the first such placement ever.

- Pepsi Top Gun national sweepstakes. The grand prize was a flight with Chuck Yeager. Other prizes included VCRs and "Top Gun" videocassettes.
- ROP ad with a high-value coupon plus the national sweepstakes entry form.
- In many markets, bottlers executed an in-store sweepstakes for a VCR or for "Top Gun" videocassettes.

TRADE

- Grocery features of the national sweepstakes at point of sale and, in many instances, an in-store sweepstakes.
- Store managers and buyers could enter a trade-only sweepstakes. The prize was the opportunity to fly with Chuck Yeager.
- Video retailers received a coupon good for a free case of Diet Pepsi with every 12 copies of "Top Gun" purchased.
- Video retailers could use a counter card featuring the Pepsi Top Gun sweepstakes to win a flight with Chuck Yeager.

RESULTS

The following were the main results of the program:
- Volume in participating markets was double that in non-participating markets.
- Pepsi Cola products received new solo distribution in nearly 10,000 video store accounts.
- Pepsi Cola Company received approximately $500,000 in free media exposure.
- Video sales of "Top Gun" exceeded all existing records.

This promotion contributed heavily to the awareness that videocassettes and video stores can be lucrative avenues for expanded sales, as long as care is taken to match the movie to the brand.

1987-88

CAMPAIGN/EVENT

Maxwell House Taste of Chicago

COMPANY

General Foods U.S.A.

BRAND

Maxwell House coffees

YEAR/AWARD

1987-88/Gold

BACKGROUND/MARKETING SITUATION

In 1987, Maxwell House enjoyed its longstanding position as the nation's best-selling coffee trademark except in Chicago, where it trailed third. The Chicago market was volatile and competitive. That year the number one coffee increased spending and the number two competitor introduced a line extension directly positioned against Maxwell House. To reach the trade and consumers, Maxwell House would have to find a way to break through the coupon clutter generated by these attacks.

OBJECTIVES

The objectives of the promotion were to increase share of market in the Chicago area, plus to increase trade merchandising in terms of feature and display activity over two periods within one quarter.

PROGRAM/STRATEGY

Maxwell House worked to gain visibility and to become more relevant to Chicago consumers by tying-in with an area event. To encourage consumer purchase, Maxwell House used a value-added offer.

Maxwell House became the official coffee sponsor for The Taste of Chicago, a city-sponsored food and entertainment festival that featured 82 booths run by area restaurants. The annual event ran for approximately one week and attracted more than 2 million people.

The program was straightforward and effective. Maxwell House set up two large coffee cafes serving regular and decaf coffee. These booths provided the only sitting areas at the festival. Consumers buying a cup of coffee at either booth received a Maxwell House coupon good for purchase at retail. In addition, Maxwell House offered a free booklet of coupons worth six dollars good at any booth at the festival. To get the booklet, consumers exchanged two empty Maxwell House coffee cans at redemption centers set up near the cafes. Two newspaper ads run a month apart included a retail coupon for Maxwell House and a coupon good for a free cup of coffee at the booths.

Support included a trade reception with Mayor Harold Washington, press releases, on-site advertising, posters, brochures, and menu advertising.

RESULTS

This promotion was a big perk for trade merchandising and market share.

- Maxwell House not only reached a record share of market for two consecutive months but also took the number one coffee position for only the second time in the history of the brand. Chicago and Peoria area shares for June rose over 100 percent; June district shares rose 60 percent; second quarter shares were 20 percent above target.
- Response to the free food booklet offer was 43,276 cans—double that expected. The cafes also exceeded traffic expectations.
- Trade results included 100 percent ACV tie-ins around the two newspaper ads. Jewel and Dominick's (comprising 60 percent of Chicago grocery trade) supported the ads with TV and ad mention. More than 30,000 cases of Maxwell House were displayed during the festival.
- The Foods Service division gained two coffee distribution points at its target accounts.
- The free publicity gained by Maxwell House was estimated by an independent agency to equal 18.7 million impressions and included radio, TV news, newspapers, magazines, coffee journals, and hotel brochures.

1987-88

CAMPAIGN/EVENT
Miller/Dragnet Sweepstakes

COMPANY
Miller Brewing Company

BRAND
Miller Genuine Draft

AGENCY
Focus Marketing Inc.

YEAR/AWARD
1987-88/Gold

BACKGROUND/MARKETING SITUATION

Miller Genuine Draft, a true draft beer purified by cold filtering instead of pasteurization, was initially introduced in 22 states in February 1987. By summer it enjoyed nationwide distribution.

The largest consumer segment for premium beers is men between the ages of 21 and 34. This segment accounts for more than half of all beer consumed. Beer sales are greatly influenced by retail display. The majority of heavy beer drinkers purchase weekly and will switch at the point-of-purchase depending on display, price, featuring, and package appeal. Thus cutting-edge advertising and promotion are needed to establish brand dominance.

OBJECTIVES

Genuine Draft was a new product, so promotional consumer and trade objectives reflected the usual goals of new product introductions—awareness and trial.

Off-premise objectives included:
• Position Genuine Draft as youthful, masculine, and contemporary.
• Generate trial and new users.
• Minimize cannibalization of the Miller High Life brand with a separate look for Genuine Draft.
• Encourage displays and motivate consumers to look for displays.

On-premise objectives included:
• Generate trial.
• Generate positive "bar talk" for the brand.

- Heighten brand awareness.
- Reinforce Genuine Draft's off-premise movie association.

PROGRAM/STRATEGY

Genuine Draft entered a joint promotion with Universal Pictures. Miller exchanged major promotional support of the movie "Dragnet" in return for the rights to utilize the likenesses of Tom Hanks and Dan Aykroyd and to offer movie props as sweepstakes prizes.

The company implemented an instant-winner 800 number sweepstakes that encouraged consumer involvement. Consumers had to look for a number on Miller cans or at a Miller Dragnet display, then call the 800 number to see if they had won.

No detail was overlooked. Point-of-sale materials included life-size images of Aykroyd and Hanks as Sergeant Joe Friday and his sidekick. A video featuring Hanks and Aykroyd was created to generate retailer enthusiasm. Major print and TV media supported the event.

RESULTS

More than 40,000 displays were placed at retail. Thousands of phone entries helped make "Dragnet" one of the top-grossing movies of 1987 and kept Genuine Draft the fastest growing brand in the beer market. Thanks to the youthful image associated with the movie, Genuine Draft continued to capture an increasing share of the market of men 21 to 34 years old.

1987-88

CAMPAIGN/EVENT

Wisk Bright Nights '87

COMPANY

Lever Brothers Company

BRAND

Wisk detergent

YEAR/AWARD

1987-88/Gold

BACKGROUND/MARKETING SITUATION

Wisk was the first liquid laundry detergent to be marketed in the United States and remained unchallenged as number one for many years. Then, between 1985 and 1987, the detergent market was inundated with liquid laundry detergent line extensions of existing powdered brands. Faced with this crowded marketplace, Wisk's plan to introduce an improved formula in celebration of its thirtieth anniversary looked less and less promising.

OBJECTIVES

In support of the restage, Lever Brothers outlined the following consumer and trade objectives.

CONSUMER

- Maintain sales despite many competitive product introductions.
- Continue as number one in the liquid detergent category.
- Communicate Wisk restage and anniversary.
- Develop community goodwill.

TRADE

- Obtain in-store support comparable to prior year.
- Develop trade goodwill.

PROGRAM/STRATEGY

Wisk developed Wisk Bright Nights '87, the first-ever fireworks tour, an integrated trade and consumer turnkey program. Bright Nights visited 23 cities across the country. This was the core of the promotion. The show consisted of a 24-minute fireworks display choreographed to music and a rock-and-roll 30-year retrospective commemorating Wisk's thirtieth anniversary. Fireworks by Grucci, Inc., the world-famous "First Family of Fireworks," executed the tour, including a special "Ring Around the Sky" fireworks shell. A few events tied-in with local celebrations, such as the We Are the People 200 Constitution festivities in Philadelphia, Venetian Nights in Chicago, and the closing of the Pan American Games in Indianapolis.

CONSUMER
- Radio simulcasts of the fireworks programs.
- Local radio and newspaper advertising.
- High-value coupons via FSI in May, June, July, and August.
- Consumer sweepstakes sending winners to the International Fireworks Competition in Monte Carlo.

TRADE
- Escalating allowances for display in consecutive summer months.
- VIP trade parties for retail supermarket buyers and their families at local shows.
- Display cards, shelf-talkers, and in-ad slicks for local radio promotion.

RESULTS

The combination of promotion and public relations set Wisk records skyrocketing:
- More than 175 million impressions were made by TV, print, and radio media.
- More than 3 million people attended the fireworks shows.
- Wisk set new sales records for 1987, not only maintaining its leadership but extending it.
- Although the category grew by only 1.5 percent, Wisk volume increased by more than 5 percent.
- Despite continued new introductions, Wisk's share of display increased by 10 percent.

Although it's hard to quantify goodwill, Lever Brothers received hundreds of thank-you letters, each a welcome surprise. It seems there's never been a fireworks display folks didn't like.

1987-88

CAMPAIGN/EVENT
Shelter Aid

COMPANY
Johnson & Johnson Consumer Products

BRANDS
Multiple brands

AGENCY
QLM Associates, Inc.

YEAR/AWARD
1987-88/Gold

BACKGROUND/MARKETING SITUATION

Participating brands from the Johnson & Johnson family of brands included Stayfree, Medipren, Sine-Aid, o.b. Tampons, PediaCare Children's Cold Relief, Johnson & Johnson's Baby Powder, REACH Toothbrush, Johnson's Baby Shampoo, and BAND-AID Brand Adhesive. All of these brands were leaders in their categories and well-known to consumers. Nevertheless, each faced a stiff competitive retail environment.

Stayfree, for example, was the leading brand in its category but was declining and had no ammunition to reverse that trend. Its category had become increasingly price and promotion driven; it had very limited advertising; competing brands had instituted product and packaging improvements it could neither match nor best.

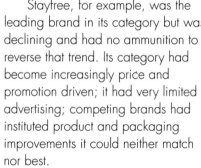

OBJECTIVES

Johnson & Johnson's general objective was to reinforce positive images for the brands and for the corporation. The shared objectives were to:
- Produce sales increases for all brands in the promotion.
- Encourage high levels of trade merchandising support.
- Generate maximum enthusiasm among sales reps in all divisions.

For Stayfree specifically, the objective was to reverse declining share and to achieve a sales bump.

PROGRAM/STRATEGY

Johnson & Johnson reasoned that a cause-related program could achieve all objectives. The concern was to find an issue that would have a strong enough social dimension to motivate consumers (primarily women) to act. Johnson & Johnson has a corporate credo that stresses that the company has a responsibility to the women and children who use their products, as well as to the communities in which they live and work. Research had indicated that women were ready to support businesses that supported any resolution to domestic violence. The issue that was chosen — domestic violence — was considered appropriate to meet these criteria.

Shelter Aid was designed to help the victims of domestic violence with:

- Funding — a donation by the sponsoring brands of $562,000—to establish and operate the first year of the first national toll-free domestic violence hotline. The hotline, staffed by the National Coalition Against Domestic Violence, allowed women to talk toll-free to people who could help immediately. This was the only national network of shelters and staff.
- Financial contributions to domestic violence shelters for women and children:
—A three-page FSI with 10 coupons was distributed nationally. For each coupon redeemed, five cents would be donated to the National Coalition Against Domestic Violence.
—A proof collection program with a five-cent donation for each proof-of-purchase submitted from Medipren or Stayfree. Special mailing envelopes were provided at point-of-sale, community centers, and shelters.
- Publicity and education:
—Kickoff with a Washington, D.C., press event attended by women's groups, political groups, and the press. A second event involved screening an episode of the TV show "Cagney & Lacey," which was the topic of a panel discussion along with Lindsay Wagner. A public service announcement spot was filmed and shown nationwide in conjunction with the episode.
—A major market media and satellite tour were also implemented.

RESULTS

The following were the results:

- All brands received significant share bumps.
- Support from all sectors was phenomenal: the trade, consumers, the sales force, the press, shelters, and women's groups.
- Donations to shelters approximated $1.5 million, the highest donation ever made to a women's issue and possibly the highest promotion donation for a single event ever made by a package goods manufacturer.
- The hotline received 20,000 calls in the first two months.

Stayfree achieved dramatic sales increases, as much as 72 percent in one category during drop, and the staying power demonstrated by a +22 share in the four weeks following the drop.

1987-88

CAMPAIGN/EVENT
The Nike Challenge

COMPANY
Nike, Inc.

BRANDS
All Nike athletic footwear

AGENCY
American Consulting Corporation

YEAR/AWARD
1987-88/Silver

BACKGROUND/MARKETING SITUATION

The athletic footwear market is highly competitive and dominated by a handful of brands. At one time, performance was the driving force behind selection, but by the mid-1980s, fashion and image had become increasingly important factors in purchase decisions. Back-to-school was one of the busiest, most fashion-conscious, and most competitive seasons of the year for athletic footwear.

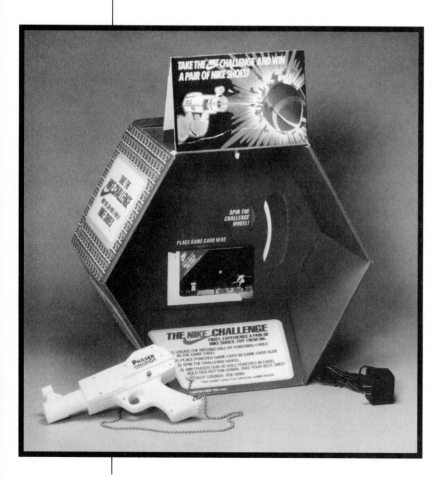

In 1987, Nike was the second largest manufacturer of athletic footwear in the United States. Having started a category explosion with the "waffled" running shoe a decade earlier, the company now introduced the Nike Air line of footwear.

OBJECTIVES

Nike recognized that the technological superiority of Nike Air alone could not sustain all footwear sales, so the company chose broad objectives:
- Generate excitement about all Nike footwear during back-to-school.
- Encourage trial (try-on) of all Nike footwear.
- Obtain broad-based retailer support of in-store promotion.

PROGRAM/STRATEGY

Nike invited America to take The Nike Challenge, an interactive in-store contest using trendy electronic phaser guns. The contest was designed to draw kids into a store to try on a pair of Nikes and to excite retailers.

The challenge was fun. In return for a try-on, the consumer received a game card marked with holes to punch. The consumer punched one hole on the card, which was then inserted into a wheel on the display. While the wheel spun, the consumer aimed the phaser at the hole and shot. An electronic beep announced a hit and a winner. Each winner received a free pair of Nikes on the spot from the retailer.

Support events to generate more response included:

- National radio tie-ins with Casey Kasem's America's Top 40.
- Distribution of game cards through a national tie-in with Gatorade, which encouraged store traffic.
- Extra phasers available to retailers at deep discounts to sell in-store or to use as a purchase-with-purchase item.
- Retail display pieces and banners.
- Co-op funds for black and white ad slicks.
- Retail clerk sweepstakes with trips to the 1988 Super Bowl for clerks. For each game card completed and signed by a consumer, the clerk had another entry into the sweepstakes.

RESULTS

Trade response was so good that display production and placements were more than twice the original estimates, in spite of the fact that approximately 500 retailers missed the opportunity to obtain display materials because they had responded too late to modify the production run. Retailer feedback was unanimously positive.

1987-88

CAMPAIGN/EVENT

Hardee's California Raisins Promotion

COMPANY

Hardee's Food Systems, Inc.

PRODUCTS

Rise & Shine biscuits and desserts

AGENCY

Ogilvy & Mather

YEAR/AWARD

1987-88/Silver

BACKGROUND/MARKETING SITUATION

In 1987, Hardee's had passed Wendy's to become the third largest hamburger fast-food chain in the United States, behind only McDonald's and Burger King. In addition to its lunch and dinner menus, Hardee's had a selection of breakfast foods.

The fast-food industry has always been intensely competitive, but by 1987 double-digit growth of the category as a whole had slowed to a mere 5 percent. Hardee's breakfast items, Rise & Shine biscuits in particular, needed a boost in sales for the short term. This could only be achieved by shifting share from the competition.

OBJECTIVES

Hardee's was most concerned about the following:
- Generating additional sales by current customers.
- Attracting new customers away from competition.
- Increasing systemwide sales by 4.5 percent during the four-week promotion period.
- Increasing breakfast and dessert sales during the month of October.

PROGRAM/STRATEGY

Since California raisins were used in Rise & Shine biscuits, Hardee's seized the opportunity to draw on the current popularity of the California Raisins characters.

The California Raisins™
Collect All Four

With the purchase of any two Rise & Shine Biscuits™ or Dessert.

California Raisins figurines were sold with the purchase of Hardee's Rise & Shine biscuits or desserts.

Awareness of the program was developed in several ways:

- Advertising: A teaser print campaign, designed to kick off the campaign, was followed by TV, radio, newsprint, and outdoor advertising.
- In-store promotion: Point-of-purchase materials included window decals, posters, tray liners, crew buttons, table tents, and motorized displays.
- Local merchandising: Contests were held on local radio to encourage the California Raisins craze.
- Appearances: The California Raisins characters made appearances in Hardee's restaurants and at local events, including the North Carolina State Fair.

RESULTS

Approximately 15 million figurines were sold during the four-week program, while October dollar sales increased 18 percent versus the prior year. Some restaurants reported 30 percent increases.

October was the largest year-to-year increase in Hardee's history. In contrast, McDonald's sales increased only 2 percent; Burger King, 6 percent; and Wendy's sales declined versus the prior year. The promotion was so popular that a Raisins hot line was created to help consumers get the figurines after they had been sold out in the restaurants. This is more evidence that a promotion's success depends upon its dynamic interaction with consumer perceived wants, not upon its complexity.

1987-88

CAMPAIGN/EVENT

Frequent Buyer

COMPANY

Food World, Inc.

BRAND

Grocery products

YEAR/AWARD

1987-88/Silver

BACKGROUND/MARKETING SITUATION

Food World, Inc., operated its 294-store Acme Supermarkets chain through a seven-state area on the East Coast. Acme's territory was riddled with soft sales, reduced tonnage, increased operating costs, eroded customer loyalty, heavy markdowns, and diminished profits. Analysis revealed that real sales growth was flat and in some instances falling off from the prior year. In this environment, a unique promotion was needed.

OBJECTIVES

Acme's problems necessitated more than a short-term "cosmetic" event. To restore customer loyalty, protect market share, attract competitors' customers, stimulate traffic, and generate sales activity, a host of objectives were outlined:

- Halt the eroding share of the market and regain original position.
- Increase tonnage.
- Tap into FSI-type funding.
- Implement a point of difference that would be difficult to duplicate in the marketplace.
- Add continuity.
- Develop a low-price image.
- Introduce an incentive program for all levels of field and store management.
- Increase employee sensitivity to consumer needs.
- Implement a promotion that would offset the cost of the program through a combination of vendor funding and the selling of weekly circular advertising space to national accounts.

PROGRAM/STRATEGY

The strategy was to transform the traditional controlled markdown program into a real value-added element that could prolong involvement on the part of the consumer. This multilevel program was implemented:

- Coupons similar to trading stamps were issued in two denominations ($1 and $10) to be given to customers based on full dollar purchases.
- Customers received free blank Frequent Buyer Cheks on which they would paste coupons. Upon accumulating $40 worth, in any combination of $1 or $10 denominations, customers could redeem filled Cheks in Acme supermarkets on Frequent Buyer food specials. In addition, customers had the option of redeeming their Cheks, worth at least $1, at any of 3,700 associated accounts. Associated account tie-ins included major fast food franchises, athletic events, car care centers, airlines, hotels, and so forth.
- Food World solicited nonprofit organizations to collect filled Frequent Buyer Cheks for their groups.
- Double stamps were issued on certain commodities (meat, produce, dairy) some days in order to build traffic in those departments.
- Acme's weekly circulars were used to promote the program and to defray the cost of the promotion by selling space to associate accounts.
- Associate accounts gave double value on all Frequent Buyer Cheks redeemed during a specified period of time.
- Featured food specials provided tie-ins offering exclusive redemption on specific brands to increase tonnage through the chain.
- Acme instituted a two-stage employee VIP card program in support of the Frequent Buyer program. In Stage 1, all employees of associated accounts got cards with double stamps for purchase on a specified day of the week. In Stage 2, Acme employees got cards enabling them to get discounts at associated accounts.
- The 26-week program was supported by heavier than usual advertising via TV, direct mail, and newspapers.

RESULTS

The following were key results:

- The program stayed in effect for two years instead of the originally planned 26 weeks.
- Acme regained three market share points.
- Associate accounts showed an increase in their average transaction.
- What originally had been a cost promotion became a profit center adding nearly 1 percent to Acme's bottom line.
- More than $4 million of Cheks were redeemed by more than 1,500 nonprofit groups at 50 cents per Chek.
- Nearly 90 percent of Acme's customers participated in the program.
- More than 70 percent of Cheks in the marketplace were redeemed.
- Vendors participating in the promotion experienced a tremendous increase in product movement.
- Traffic count was up by more than 3 percent.
- The average transaction was increased by nearly 12 percent.
- The promotion gave Acme the low-price image it desired.
- More than $2.2 million worth of ads were sold for the weekly circular inserts to associate accounts.

This program added value to the customer's purchase, broadened the appeal through redemption at associate accounts, and was cost-efficient because most redemption was absorbed by the tie-in partners.

1987-88

CAMPAIGN/EVENT

Play Monopoly at McDonald's game

COMPANY

McDonald's Corporation

BRAND

McDLT sandwich

AGENCY

Simon Marketing, Inc.

YEAR/AWARD

1987-88/Silver

BACKGROUND/MARKETING SITUATION

In the Spring of 1987, the opportunity existed for McDonald's to enhance its leadership role in the fast food (or quick service restaurant) industry. In the second quarter of each year, the quick service restaurant business generally increases as weather improves and consumer lifestyles become more active. By promoting aggressively in April and May, McDonald's hoped to capture those additional customers and to maintain the momentum of increased traffic and sales into the summer.

OBJECTIVES

McDonald's aimed for increases in three areas:
- Customer traffic.
- Trial of the McDLT sandwich, a part of McDonald's new product introduction program.
- Sales per store.

PROGRAM/STRATEGY

The strategy was to tie-in to Monopoly, America's most recognized and longest selling game, and thus to draw people into McDonald's restaurants with rewards for playing Monopoly at McDonald's.

Monopoly at McDonald's was an exciting stamp collection game

that gave consumers the opportunity to win big prizes (cars, cash, homes, vacations) either instantly or by collecting the stamps. Game pieces were distributed during a six-week promotion period. The game was structured similar to Monopoly. Individual stamps gave the consumer the chance to collect "deeds" to places on a modified Monopoly board or to receive Chance and Community Chest cards. Instant winners were seeded heavily through the cards, especially with McDLT sandwiches.

RESULTS

The program produced double-digit sales and transaction increases, approximately twice the forecast for the program. (Other results of the program were confidential.) This promotion generated outstanding visibility because it represented a perfect match between two classic icons—Monopoly and McDonald's—both ubiquitous to American culture.

1988-1989

REGGIE

AWARDS

CAMPAIGNS

SEND THE FAMILIES/AMERICAN TEAM FAMILY FUND PROGRAM — JOSEPH E. SEAGRAM & SONS

MENNEN TOYS FOR TOTS — THE MENNEN COMPANY

SINGIN' IN THE SHOWER — LEVER BROTHERS COMPANY

THE FLINTSTONES FAMILY PROGRAM — DENNY'S INC.

BETTER AIR — TOTAL PETROLEUM, INC./VICKERS GAS STATIONS

TASTE THE MEAT...THE SAUCE...THE FLAVOR — KRAFT GENERAL FOODS, INC.

FRISKIES LOST PET SERVICE — CARNATION COMPANY

CITICORP SAVINGS SATISFACTION PROGRAM — CITICORP

COCA-COLA PRESENTS LIVE AT THE HARD ROCK CAFE — COCA-COLA USA

BANK FOR KIDS — REPUBLIC BANK OF NEW YORK CORPORATION

1988-89

CAMPAIGN/EVENT

Send the Families/American Team Family Fund Program

COMPANY

Joseph E. Seagram & Sons

BRAND

Seagram's Coolers

YEAR/AWARD

1988-89/Gold/Super Reggie

BACKGROUND/MARKETING SITUATION

Joseph E. Seagram & Sons marketed Seagram's Wine Coolers (Seagram's Coolers) nationally with consumer-driven programs. With careful marketing strategy and a product appealing to consumer tastes, the coolers gained category leadership in 1987.

Spring 1988 found the highly competitive cooler category growing strong. The year before, Bartles & Jaymes had launched a full assault on Seagram's proprietary flavors with its own line of fruit-flavored coolers. By April 1988, with the peak summer season approaching, Seagram's Coolers were holding the number one market share position with 33.3 percent, but Bartles & Jaymes was close behind at 31.3 percent. A share battle was in full swing.

OBJECTIVE

The overall objective was trade and consumer involvement that would expand market share at the expense of key competitors like Bartles & Jaymes. More specific marketing aims supported this umbrella objective.

TRADE

- Drive displays and feature ad activity during the peak selling season.
- Generate continued trade enthusiasm throughout the peak selling season.
- Enhance the broad-based leadership presence of Seagram's Coolers.

CONSUMER

- Drive continuity of purchase.
- Generate multiple purchases.

- Develop increased product usage occasions.
- Enhance Seagram's leadership position.

PROGRAM/STRATEGY

Seagram envisioned an innovative continuity program that would hold national interest. To do so, the Seagram's Coolers Send the Families/American Team Family Fund Program was created. The fund would eventually send 500 family members of the 1988 U.S. Summer Olympics team athletes to Seoul, South Korea, to share in the experience of the games.

An Advisory Board was formed, including former Olympians, members of Congress, members of U.S. sports federations, Seagram's executives, and participating distributors, to ensure the program would be the best it could be.

Advertising of $5.5 million positioned Seagram's Coolers as the exclusive wine cooler sponsor of the NBC-TV Summer Olympics telecast. TV advertising focused flights on prime sales periods of the peak season—Memorial Day, July 4th, and Labor Day—directing consumers to participating stores to take part in the program.

As part of the public relations program, the world's largest Bon Voyage card traveled from coast to coast, stopping in 30 cities for signatures. During September in Los Angeles, the card was the centerpiece for the Bon Voyage family send-off party to Seoul.

TRADE
- Mini Bon Voyage cards.
- Shelf materials and posters.
- Consumer brochures.
- TV viewing guides.
- Refund carton stuffers.
- Decal case card Bon Voyage card announcements (to participating retailers).
- Taverns, lounges, and restaurants received table tents, counter cards holding take-one brochures, and TV viewing guides, while United Airlines and Marriott received special custom-designed merchandising materials and programs.

Seagram used a sales video to motivate its distributors and customized materials for national accounts wishing to tie into the program.

CONSUMER
- Memorial Day
—Offer-with-purchase of Send the Families fine-art Olympic posters.
—Free take-one brochures outlining the program and an offer of commemorative merchandise (proceeds to be donated to the program).
—Contributor decal for all consumers who contributed to the program.
- July 4th
—Featured consumer rebate with savings up to $4 on cases and half-cases of Seagram's Coolers.
—Opportunity to donate all or part of the rebate to the Send the Families program.
- Labor Day
—Free take-one Seagram's Summer Games TV viewing guide.

RESULTS

Send the Families received enthusiastic support from all major media. Newspapers, magazines, primetime news, and cable news picked up the story. Nearly 400 million impressions were delivered, valued between $7 million and $10 million.

As measured by Nielsen ScanTrack, trade feature and ad display from May into October surpassed prior-year activity in all but two instances. Increases averaged more than 20 percent and in some cases were up by more than 30 percent. In addition, more than 100 distributors contributed $100,000 to the fund.

Approximately 140,000 consumers participated in the case rebate program, and average take-away increased by more than three four-packs per purchase. This led Seagram's Coolers sales to exceed category performance rates, indexing at 103 on ScanTrack.

This promotion also scored high on personal satisfaction for all those involved in its execution. The Big Card Tour eventually sent hundreds of signatures, written on the Bon Voyage cards, displays, and table tents to the Olympic athletes and their families. Fourteen mayors and two governors co-hosted the Bon Voyage party attended by special guests, political dignitaries, and former Olympians. It showed that good promotion and goodwill need not be mutually exclusive.

1988-89

CAMPAIGN/EVENT

Mennen Toys For Tots

COMPANY

The Mennen Company

BRANDS

Speed Stick deodorants, Baby Magic products

YEAR/AWARD

1988-89/Gold

BACKGROUND/MARKETING SITUATION

Growth of a number of Mennen brands (Speed Stick Deodorant, Anti-Perspirant Deodorant, Lady Speed Dry Anti-Perspirant, Lady Speed Stick Anti-Perspirant, Baby Magic Baby Lotion, and Baby Magic Baby Oil) had been substantial through the 1980s, but slowed in 1988. Several factors were responsible:

- Mennen virtually eliminated promotional activity on deodorants for the fourth quarter of 1987.
- Activity—product introductions and restaging, plus heavy spending—by competing brands constituted some of the most significant increases in history.

The fourth quarter 1988 was now critical for Mennen. It promised larger budget expenditures, represented a chance to overcome shortages from the early part of the year, and provided the base for getting a head start on 1989. The use of floor displays would be crucial for success, but, unfortunately, there was a tradition of bias against floor displays for health and beauty aids at this time of the year. The trade preferred holiday season displays.

OBJECTIVE

Mennen needed a program that would appeal to consumers and convince the trade to forego existing seasonal promotions in favor of ad and feature display for Mennen products.

PROGRAM/STRATEGY

The strategy was to use the U.S. Marine Toys For Tots program as a timely, cause-related vehicle that would be desirable and readily identifiable by everyone (both consumer and trade). The program consisted of:

- A significant donation of toys ($200,000 retail value in toys) as Mennen's contribution to the cause.
- A two-page FSI offering high-value coupons on all participating Mennen brands.
- FSI recognition for Hasbro, as the manufacturer of the toys being contributed, in return for a discount on the purchase of the toys.
- Trade tie-ins offered stores the opportunity to participate as collection centers for the Toys For Tots program utilizing collection bins and posters provided by Mennen.
- Almost 5,000 Mennen Toys For Tots collection bins placed in stores.
- Trade recognition awards for those retailers who gave significant support to the program.
- Help from U.S. Marine Reserves personnel from 250 reserve sites, who accompanied Mennen sales reps on their calls.

RESULTS

Sales of participating brands grew 12 percent from the prior year. Despite competition from holiday season displays, trade response rose dramatically, with significant increases in both ad and floor displays. Ad feature performance was 15 to 20 percent better than the previous year.

This event generated some noteworthy support from retailers, several of whom tied-in their own Toys For Tots events with Mennen's. Kroger Atlanta Division timed Santa's arrival by helicopter to coincide with a children's toy donation day. Drug Emporium in Philadelphia kicked off Mennen Toys For Tots with in-store appearances of the Philadelphia Eagles' Cheerleaders and the U.S. Marines. They offered a $5 coupon on the consumer's next Drug Emporium purchase if the toy donation had a value of $15 or more. These and more individual "supporting" stories around the nation demonstrated how an event can be simultaneously socially responsible and profitable.

1988-89

CAMPAIGN/EVENT

Singin' in the Shower

COMPANY

Lever Brothers Company

BRANDS

Multiple brand bar soaps

AGENCY

Contemporary Group

YEAR/AWARD

1988-89/Gold

BACKGROUND/MARKETING SITUATION

The Lever Brothers bar soap category included five of the country's leading and most recognized brands: Caress, Lux, Lifebuoy, Shield, and Dove (ranked first for dollar-share). The bar soap category was crowded with over 15 national brands, and competition for shelf space was extremely intense. Category activity was characterized by frequent line extensions, multi-packs, on-pack offers, and extensive consumer and trade promotion spending. Display space was difficult to leverage. Retailers reserved almost all space for new product introductions or price-point promotions. Incremental displays, which translated into incremental consumer sales, were crucial for dominance in this retail arena.

OBJECTIVES

These were the four objectives for the promotion:

- Obtain a greater number of displays in the key summer selling months, April through August, primarily in the grocery and mass merchandiser classes of trade.
- Generate increased purchase and continuity of purchase among users.
- Generate awareness of Lever bar soaps among consumers in general.
- Develop an event that would establish an ownership for Lever's brands; i.e., a yearly event that consumers would identify with the brand names.

SINGIN' IN THE SHOWER

A Clean Promotion
That'll Soak Up Listeners!

PROGRAM/STRATEGY

Lever's strategy was to develop a fully integrated promotion that supported the participating bar soap brands and addressed both consumer and trade objectives. It would also achieve extended media reach and would encourage public relations activity. To do so, Lever implemented the following three-phase contest and sweepstakes program.

PHASE 1: SPECIAL EVENT PROMOTION

From May 1 through May 15, the Singin' in the Shower contest was launched via radio stations in 30 markets. Contest participants sang their shower songs over the air. Songs had to incorporate Lever bar soap brand names and the radio station I.D. into the lyrics. Prizes, including trips to Dunn's River Falls in Jamaica and "clean-up" kits (a shower radio, soap, scrub brush, rubber duck), were supplied by Lever in exchange for media mentions.

PHASE 2: LIVE EVENT

From June through September, all Phase 1 radio stations hosted a live Shower contest. Three transportable Singin' in the Shower sets were constructed and moved from market to market. Eight to 10 individual contestants or singing groups in each market were selected to perform "in the tub." Lever provided a trip to Hollywood and cash prizes to local market winners. A radio station provided media support and an on-air personality at each event in exchange for co-sponsorship of the event, event production expenses, and prizes.

PHASE 3: NATIONAL FINALS

First-place winners from all markets were flown to Universal Studios Tour Theme Park in Hollywood for a national final Shower on October 1.

RELATED ACTIVITIES

A point-of-sale sweepstakes display, a sales video, and collateral materials were produced for the sales force and the trade. In addition, the standard tower for product display was enlarged and modified to resemble a shower stall. Inside, a consumer-activated voice box "sang" a contest jingle. The display carried entry forms for a national sweepstakes and directed consumers to local radio stations that would run a Singin' in the Shower contest.

For the consumer promotion, each of the participating Lever bar soaps dropped national FSI and direct mail offers during key promotion months. Offers included cash refunds and coupons.

Publicity included press kits, media alerts, and followup supporting the national rollout. The top 15 markets received on-site management and coverage.

RESULTS

Universal Studios advertised the finals with signage throughout the park, and the finals were so well received that CBS and ABC each gave the event network coverage. In all, the publicity earned by Singin' in the Shower included 6.4 million print circulation and 10.6 million television viewership. (Something to sing about!)

In addition, the sweepstakes generated an unprecedented 10 percent response. Lever Brothers leveraged more than $750,000 in promotional media from the 30 participating radio stations. It netted a 5 to 1 return on expenditures and gained 87 million gross impressions. Singin' in the Shower events were held at premier locations throughout the country, from the Seattle State Fair to Broadway in downtown Manhattan. Not surprisingly, Lever became the number one displayed company during the promotional period.

1988-89

CAMPAIGN/EVENT

The Flintstones Family Program

COMPANY

Denny's, Inc.

BRAND

Family restaurant

AGENCY

Strottman Marketing, Inc.

YEAR/AWARD

1988-89/Gold

BACKGROUND/MARKETING SITUATION

The family or mid-scale restaurant segment offers complete table service and a broad variety of menu items at relatively low prices. It is primarily a local business, with local tastes, customs, habits, and economic conditions exerting the dominant influence on a restaurant's success or failure. Denny's was the leader in this segment, as the only truly national chain of its kind. Much of its strongest competition was in individual or regional markets where single-city or regional chains are active.

Denny's business had been soft for more than 18 months (since 1986). Children are a key influence on family dining habits, but Denny's single, short-term promotions had not been enough to change children's tastes and make Denny's their restaurant of choice. Meanwhile, heavily advertised, ongoing promotional efforts to children by fast food restaurants had created the need to offer families continuing incentives to come to Denny's. Yet Denny's had no such long-term program in operation.

OBJECTIVES

The Denny's Flintstones Family Program was designed to meet three objectives:

- Improve overall sales and profitability but avoid food discounting, thus protecting Denny's reputation for good quality food and service.
- Increase guest counts by at least 5 percent in the segment of families with children under age 10.
- Achieve long-term penetration of the family segment and establish Denny's as the restaurant of choice for families.

PROGRAM/STRATEGY

Denny's chose to develop The Flintstones Family Program as a year-long family program to increase the number and frequency of family visits. The Flintstones were selected because they represented a strong, positive family image and have been enormously popular for more than 30 years with people of all ages, especially with children.

TRADE

At the trade, or individual, restaurant level, Denny's restaurant operators had never implemented a year-long promotion. So training and support materials about comprehensive children's marketing were developed:

- A Denny's "Bedrock News" newsletter.
- A Flintstones program folder.
- Ad materials.
- Crew buttons.

CONSUMER

The consumer program encompassed four areas:

- Premiums: four sets of premiums were developed for seasonal selling points throughout the year:
—Cuddly plush Flintstones Friends toys—eight-inch toys of all the Flintstones characters.
—Flintstones Collector Series plates—classic Flintstones scenes illustrated on high-quality plastic plates.
—Flintstones reusable placemats—Flintstones scenes on one side and games and activities on the other.
—Flintstones lunch boxes.
- Menu: Denny's designed a special children's menu incorporating the Flintstones theme with the most popular foods. The menu gave new names to traditional children's meals (e.g., Brontosaurus Burger). It featured colorful characters and scenes on both sides.
- Activity Books: a series of 12 monthly activity books was developed to entertain kids while they waited for food. Each book featured a Flintstones story along with games, puzzles, and jokes. New books released each month encouraged repeat visits.
- Birthdays: the Flintstones/Denny's Birthday Club made one day extra special for the birthday child. Custom birthday cards were mailed to children just before their birthdays, entitling each child to a free children's meal and a birthday sundae.

ADVERTISING SUPPORT

The premiums were supported by Denny's first-ever television effort. The entire program included:

- :30 TV spots.
- :60 radio commercials.
- Newspaper ads.
- An extensive point-of-sale kit that contained counter cards, table tents, posters, and banners.
- Flintstones costume character tour featuring Fred, Barney, and Dino.

RESULTS

Trade support was unanimous, and the reasons were clear:

- Customer traffic objectives were exceeded. Total guest counts increased by 6 percent or more in all markets.
- Net sales increased by more than 6 percent.
- Profitability increases were in the double digits—beyond Denny's wildest dreams!

1988-89

CAMPAIGN/EVENT
Better Air

COMPANY
Total Petroleum, Inc./Vickers Gas Stations

BRAND
Vickers gasoline

AGENCY
Barnhart Advertising

YEAR/AWARD
1988-89/Gold

BACKGROUND/MARKETING SITUATION

Total Petroleum, Inc., was an independent oil company headquartered in Denver. It sold its gasoline products under the Vickers and Total brand names through the Midwest. Operating approximately 50 self-service gas stations in the Denver metropolitan area under the Vickers brand name, it was one of the largest retailers of gasoline in the region.

Total shared in the criticism directed at Denver-area petroleum companies for their perceived resistance to Denver's Better Air campaign. Total determined that the company would need to take a more proactive role within the community if it was to overcome this negative image. Late in 1987, the company developed a six-week promotion designed to encourage the citizens of Denver to support the city's drive for cleaner air.

OBJECTIVES

Total had a dual focus for the program. For the city of Denver there were two objectives:

- Generate increased awareness of the Better Air campaign.
- Generate increased bus ridership during the Better Air campaign.

For Vickers there were three:

- Increase awareness of Vickers as a responsible corporate citizen.

- Increase awareness of the Vickers brand name.
- Generate increased gasoline sales during 1989.

PROGRAM/STRATEGY

Since the Better Air campaign already had a "no-drive" component, which asked Denver citizens to leave their cars home for one day a week, Total developed a program that encouraged consumers to use the Regional Transportation District (RTD) bus system on those days. The program included the following:

- Free round-trip bus coupons for any route served by the RTD given to customers who filled their gas tanks at any participating Vickers gas station.
- A comprehensive media kit that included information about the promotion, a list of participating gas stations, photos, bus coupons, and a fact sheet about the Better Air campaign.
- A four-week radio campaign featuring a :60 radio spot that announced Vickers' support of the Better Air campaign and the Vickers program, then encouraged Denver citizens to support the program as well.
- Additional point-of-sale materials, including station banners, counter displays, and buttons for all employees.
- A public relations campaign directed at local, regional, and national media, plus the trade.

In addition, to support the program among Total's 850 employees, management distributed free bus coupons and encouraged corporate personnel to participate in the Better Air campaign.

A kickoff meeting with all Vickers station managers and supervisory personnel introduced the program and stressed the need for support. Representatives of the Better Air campaign and the RTD gave station managers additional collateral material to help answer consumer questions about the program and the campaign.

RESULTS

The program was promoted as the first time a petroleum company had asked its customers to drive less to help clean up the air, so this unusual event drew extensive media coverage. Favorable consumer perception of Total moved from 43 percent in a 1986 study to 49 percent in 1988. Total Petroleum/Vickers was honored by the Better Air campaign and received special recognition from the governor of Colorado. All TV stations and 16 radio stations covered the event. Over 120,000 free ride coupons were given away during the six-week program. More than 60,000 were redeemed by RTD, and bus ridership increased 14 percent over the previous year. Despite a major snow storm that kept people off the roads during late December, Vickers recorded significant gasoline sales increases during December and January.

1988-89

CAMPAIGN/EVENT

Taste the Meat...the Sauce...the Flavor

COMPANY

Kraft General Foods, Inc.

BRANDS

Bull's-Eye Barbecue Sauce and America's Cut Pork

YEAR/AWARD

1988-89/Gold

BACKGROUND/MARKETING SITUATION

Bull's-Eye Barbecue Sauce, a premium sauce developed by Kraft, was introduced in 1985. By 1988, it enjoyed a 6.5 percent share of the barbecue sauce category and was responsible for growth in the premium segment of the category.

Barbecue sauce is primarily a seasonal product. Approximately 60 percent of consumption occurs between April and August, with Memorial Day being the key period. Consumers purchase approximately two bottles of barbecue sauce per season, making the first purchase decision critical to success for the season. Competitive pressure is fierce.

Because sampling proved very effective for Bull's-Eye during introduction, Kraft wished to continue sampling in those markets where further development was needed. Realizing that the ideal sampling arena is right in the grocery store where the consumer can make an immediate purchase, Kraft sought a sampling method that would be both cost-effective and efficient.

OBJECTIVES

The key objective was to increase awareness and trial of Bull's-Eye with both consumers and the trade. It was critical to gain trial early in the season so that consumers would taste the product well before Memorial Day. An equally important objective was to gain feature ads and cross-merchandising in the meat department.

PROGRAM/STRATEGY

Research had indicated that consumer consumption of pork had increased in recent years due to the lower fat and cholesterol content of today's pork. Also, pork represented 31 percent of all meat consumption and was second only to chicken for barbecues.

Kraft proposed a joint promotion to the National Pork Producers Council to capitalize on the efficiencies inherent in this kind of tie-in. The Pork Council agreed to help Kraft convince meat managers to insert sample packets of Bull's-Eye inside packages of America's Cut Pork.

The merchandising program was extensive and flexible:

- Accounts could distribute either a 2.5 ounce packet of Bull's-Eye or a 20¢ instant coupon inside packages of America's Cut.
- A co-op fund was established for accounts agreeing to feature America's Cut and Bull's-Eye in Best Food Day Meat ads.
- The promotion theme Taste the Meat...the Sauce...the Flavor was carried through for all point-of-sale materials.
- Two retailer kits, one for sampling and one for coupons, were developed.
- The Council and the Kraft sales force collaborated on joint sales effort. Samples and point-of-sale materials were shipped directly to account warehouses, thus freeing the sales force from the logistics of implementation.
- Samples were wrapped with cuts of pork on meat trays, then stickered with custom Bull's-Eye/America's Cut recipe labels and a "free sample" burst. Bull's-Eye displays were placed in or near the meat case.

RESULTS

The promotion was tremendously successful:

- More than 2.5 million samples were distributed.
- Of the 40 major participating accounts, approximately 75 percent in-packed samples rather than coupons, and more than 90 percent fulfilled program guidelines to qualify for co-op funding.
- Bull's-Eye exceeded yearly tonnage goals by more than 50 percent.
- In some markets, Bull's-Eye sales were up 200 percent.
- America's Cut tonnage more than doubled that of the previous year.
- The Pork Council was contacted by accounts asking how they might participate in similar programs.

This tie-in worked for Bull's-Eye because the Pork Council already had a firm relationship with account meat managers. In turn, it benefited the Pork Council because it offered an added-value, attention-getting device to promote their new trademarked pork chop. More significantly, this promotion generated such goodwill among consumers for both tie-in partners, that it was repeated in 1989 and expanded to 65 accounts in 22 markets.

1988-89

CAMPAIGN/EVENT
Friskies Lost Pet Service

COMPANY
Carnation Company

BRANDS
Friskies, Fancy Feast, Perform, Acclaim dry and canned pet foods

YEAR/AWARD
1988-89/Gold

BACKGROUND/MARKETING SITUATION

Friskies pet care products held leading positions in their respective categories. Five of the six brands were in the top 5 percent of best-selling dry grocery products. Exceptional brand awareness made them natural items to draw attention to a cause or event.

Despite its leadership position, Friskies faced intense and continuous competition from branded and generic pet foods. Brand loyalty in the subcategories (e.g., canned, dry, dog, cat) is low, resulting in brand switching driven by heavy promotion spending. Pet food is a highly promotable category with shoppers making daily or weekly purchases. Maintaining brand awareness is the key to holding the leadership position. Friskies was challenged to develop a promotion that broke through the clutter with a compelling and unique reason to purchase Friskies products.

OBJECTIVES

The primary consumer objective was to maximize coupon redemption for all brands.

The secondary consumer objective was to generate goodwill and loyalty with pet owners and then to use the goodwill program to develop a direct marketing database of customers.

The primary trade objective was to get more feature displays and ads that would drive increased volume for all Friskies brands.

PROGRAM/STRATEGY

Friskies structured a promotion that would appeal to all pet owners by serving their needs in a compelling way. The result was the Friskies Lost Pet Service.

The Friskies Lost Pet Service offered consumers across America some hope for finding lost animals. Although losing a pet can have a traumatic effect on its owner, there was no national service of this kind in existence. The service was a network of caring professionals trained to help recover lost pets. Tied into an extensive computer system, it could check animal shelters, humane societies, and rescue facilities within 60 miles of where a pet was lost. It offered other advantages as well: a 24-hour toll-free hotline, pet care information, a personalized pet I.D. tag, and coupons for Friskies pet care products and Carnation products.

To announce the program to consumers, Friskies utilized a two-page national FSI, ROP, and magazine ads targeted to specific product audiences (cats or dogs), direct mail, and on-pack coupons. A separate trade incentive program to get increased feature and displays for all Friskies brands was also developed.

RESULTS

The goal for consumer enrollment was met, while volume objectives for the division were surpassed. One brand shipped a record number of cases, and more retailers featured Friskies brands on display and in ads than any other multi-pet food promotion the company had ever run.

1988-89

CAMPAIGN/EVENT

Citicorp Savings Satisfaction Program

COMPANY

Citicorp

BRAND

Citicorp financial services

AGENCY

QLM Associates, Inc.

YEAR/AWARD

1988-89/Gold

BACKGROUND/MARKETING SITUATION

In 1988, Citicorp Savings of California was owned by Citicorp, but operated independently as a savings and loan. It was relatively new to California, where competition in the retail banking business was keen and customer service standards relatively high. Most major banks advertised in broadcast, outdoor media, and print, but Citicorp did not.

Citicorp Savings had an internal program called Service Excellence. Surveys indicated that the program and management's continued commitment to service excellence had produced an 85 percent customer satisfaction level. It was determined that concentration on problem avoidance and problem resolution would help reduce the number of dissatisfied customers and win over a number of "neutrals."

OBJECTIVES

Internal objectives were to:
- Educate personnel in branches and elsewhere about the importance of complaint resolution to each individual and to Citicorp Savings.
- Motivate personnel to provide the finest in courteous problem solving available to bank customers.
- Heighten employee awareness and action to prevent problems before they arise.

Customer objectives were to:
- Provide fast, effective resolution of customer problems and complaints.
- Re-establish a positive attitude toward the bank among customers who had had problems resolved.
- Raise customer awareness of the

organization's commitment to exceptional service and quick complaint resolution.

PROGRAM/STRATEGY

A two-faceted program—one for internal needs and one for customers—was developed.

INTERNAL PROGRAM

The theme for the program, Join the Satisfaction Team, was delivered by a teaser campaign. Teaser mentions appeared in the employee newsletter with followup by teaser posters. The program was officially launched at a semi-annual employee meeting.

Employees were provided pledge cards to sign and to make a commitment to providing exceptional service, preventing customer problems, and resolving problems that did arise. This pledge was displayed in a Plexiglas holder on each employee's desk. The symbol of "thumbs up" was developed as the logo for the campaign. All branch employees were instructed that they must treat other employees like customers. A videotape was developed and used for training.

Collateral tools were developed to assist employees in problem resolution and followup:
- Satisfaction Request Form: The customer was given a copy of the form as assurance that something tangible and positive was being done to resolve a problem.
- Tickler File: Satisfaction Request Forms were filed in a desktop reminder file. Each form was to be filed beyond its respective date for action/resolution and followup call to the customer.

An employee could earn "thumbs up" credits that could earn them gifts from a catalog. All employees were given three green thumbs up awards to give to fellow employees for having given exceptional help resolving a problem. Supervisors were given additional awards to give to exceptional employees for the same purpose.

CUSTOMER PROGRAM

The program was announced to bank customers through a direct mail piece that contained three items:
- A letter from the president explaining the promotion.
- A letter explaining the Satisfaction Request Form.
- A "thumbs up" brochure with two blue "thumbs up" certificates. Customers were asked to award them to employees who gave exceptional service.

RESULTS

During the first 10 weeks of the promotion, customer response in northern California was 86 percent positive; in southern California, 56 percent positive.

Response regarding assistance from support departments was 77 percent positive in northern California and 75 percent positive in southern California. Overall satisfaction with branch problem resolution was 90 percent positive in May and 100 percent positive in June. Customers made numerous requests for more "thumbs up" certificates to give to bank employees. Many customers sent certificates to the bank president for offering the program.

1988-89

CAMPAIGN/EVENT
Coca-Cola Presents "LIVE at the Hard Rock Cafe"

COMPANY
Coca-Cola USA

BRAND
Coca-Cola® classic

YEAR/AWARD
1988-89/Gold

BACKGROUND/MARKETING SITUATION

In the multibillion-dollar soft drink industry, each share point represents millions of dollars in sales for a brand. One of the most important battles in the "cola wars" is the fight for supremacy during the peak summer season. The target audience is the youth market, and the battlefield is the supermarket. In 1988, Coca-Cola needed an event that would generate maximum interest in Coca-Cola® classic and would capture the youth market throughout that summer.

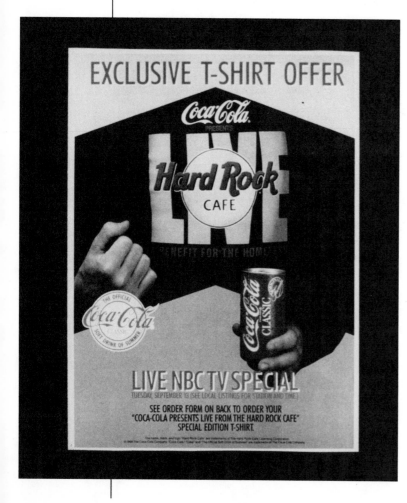

OBJECTIVE

The primary objective of the program was to further widen the gap between Coca-Cola® classic and its nearest competitor by:
- Enhancing the image and increasing youth market sales of Coca-Cola® classic.
- Increasing the size and duration of displays of Coca-Cola® classic through Labor Day.

PROGRAM/STRATEGY

Coca-Cola developed a fully integrated promotion that combined event marketing with interests most important to the youth market: music, recreation, and beachfront activities. The umbrella theme for this program, "The Official Soft Drink of Summer," was tied to one of popular music's most enduring icons: the Hard Rock Cafe.

The promotion elements included:
- Exclusive premium offer.
- Network television offer.

- National FSI.
- National television advertising.
- National publicity campaign.
- Local radio merchandising/sweepstakes.
- Point-of-sale materials.
- Bottler video.

In a grand finale to the summer, Coca-Cola sponsored a network television special broadcast, "LIVE at the Hard Rock Cafe," during the Labor Day holiday sales period. The special was dedicated to raising funds to help the homeless in America.

CONSUMERS

- Local radio sweepstakes: Consumers got the chance to win trips to the television special and commemorative T-shirts by entering a radio sweepstakes conducted by the leading radio stations in their market.
- Product purchase: Portions of the sales of Coca-Cola products were donated to benefit the homeless.
- T-shirt purchase: Through the mail, consumers purchased T-shirts commemorating the TV special. Proceeds for T-shirt sales were donated to benefit the homeless.

TRADE

- Offered special 20- and 40-case spot displays to support the program. These promoted the TV special and carried order forms for T-shirts.
- Offered commemorative sweat shirts and jean jackets as dealer loader premiums.

RESULTS

The promotion was measured as an unqualified success according to the following criteria:
- Product sales: There was a 13 percent increase in product sales during the promotion period.
- Display activity: Retailers in 80 percent of the territories served by Coca-Cola bottlers supported the promotion with product displays.
- T-shirt sales: Approximately 500,000 commemorative T-shirts were sold. Prior to this offer, the only way to purchase Hard Rock Cafe trademark identified merchandise had been to visit a Hard Rock Cafe.

1988-89

CAMPAIGN/EVENT
Bank for Kids

COMPANY
Republic New York Corporation

BRAND
Republic Bank financial services

AGENCY
The Marketing Department, Inc.

YEAR/AWARD
1988-89/Gold

BACKGROUND/MARKETING SITUATION

In 1986, Republic New York Corporation, the holding company for Republic National Bank, the seventeenth largest commercial bank in the United States, acquired Williamsburgh Savings Bank, one of the largest thrift institutions in the New York area. This acquisition meant that consumer business was now a significantly larger portion of the bank's total holdings and created the need to develop a more distinctive presence in the communities the banks served, a presence that would attract new customers.

OBJECTIVES

The promotion had five objectives:
- Switch primary focus to consumer market segments rather than on product lines.
- Demonstrate the bank's sincere interest in its customers and their financial concerns.
- Build customer loyalty.
- Win new consumer and commercial accounts.
- Distinguish the bank from its competition.

PROGRAM/STRATEGY

Actions speak louder than words. Republic conceived a plan that would be a definitive public demonstration of the bank's commitment to the stability and future growth of the community. Republic introduced the Bank for Kids.

The Bank for Kids was a bank-within-a-bank, created especially for children up to age 17. The Bank for Kids teller (a bank retiree) served children exclusively during extended kids' banking hours after 3 p.m. on Wednesdays and

Saturdays. Included in the self-contained facility were banking games, a computer, and an interactive video that taught kids about the value of saving. Kids were even issued their own make-believe ATM cards, which gave them entrance to the facility.

The Bank for Kids was launched with a well-publicized four-week back-to-school sweepstakes in a Long Island mall. Prizes included instant prizes, a twice-weekly drawing for $25 gift certificates at participating mall merchants, and six grand prizes including a $500 shopping spree.

Merchants participated by providing Bank for Kids signage. This included a lifesize cutout of Billy, the Bank for Kids "spokeskid," equipped with a customer-activated voice box so that Billy could describe the sweepstakes. Merchants also gave away Bank for Kids shopping bags. Kids could receive Bank for Kids buttons with their own pictures on them by presenting the bank a receipt for $25 or more spent at a participating merchant. Merchants received listings in all Bank for Kids printed materials.

RESULTS

The following were the results:
- Thousands of kids' accounts were opened during the promotion, exceeding objectives by more than 200 percent.
- More than 15 percent of kids' accounts generated new accounts opened by parents.
- Nearly one quarter of the mall merchants participated in the promotion.
- One quarter of the participating merchants opened commercial accounts with the bank.
- The Bank for Kids was expanded into 30 percent of the branches in the bank's system.
- The bank received regional and national press recognition.

1989-1990

REGGIE

AWARDS

CAMPAIGNS

Get Ready Giveaway — CBS/Kmart Corporation

Mattel Kids Care Too — Mattel, Inc.

Eagle Squadron — Eagle Electric Manufacturing Company

Sign On, Cash In Game — Prodigy Services Company

McDonald's Menu Song — McDonald's Corporation

Our Treat — VISA U.S.A. Inc.

SuperBowl XXIII 3-D — Coca-Cola USA

Free Pictionary Game — Kraft General Foods, Inc.

Bank South Kroger Cash Club — Bank South and Kroger Food Stores

Burger King Kids Club — Burger King Corporation

1989-90

CAMPAIGN/EVENT
Get Ready Giveaway

COMPANIES
CBS/Kmart Corporation

BRAND
CBS entertainment; Kmart shopping

YEAR
1989-90/Super Reggie

BACKGROUND/MARKETING SITUATION

CBS was lagging in third place as one of the "big three" television networks. Kmart was the nation's largest retailer in traffic and coverage, with 2,275 stores and 76 million shoppers a month.

CBS had lost viewership in the television marketplace due to changes precipitated by a proliferation of entertainment alternatives, including cable, VCRs, satellite communication, home videos, and independent television. Compounding this, the 1988 television writers' strike cost the networks their traditional fall premiere period. A proactive progressive marketing plan was needed for the fall premiere period, especially since the failure rate for new television programs is 75 percent.

Kmart, a leader in the mass merchandising industry, knew that its only constant was change. It was attempting to create novel in-store environments that added to the shopping experience. Through joint promotion marketing ventures with celebrities, Kmart was also making a successful start at upgrading consumer perceptions.

OBJECTIVES

The objectives for CBS were to:
- Generate new program sampling.
- Create more excitement for the fall season, both nationally and in CBS's 200-plus affiliate markets.

- Generate broad reach and early awareness of new programs premiering on the network.
  For Kmart, the objectives were to:
- Enhance Kmart's image even further by continuing the existing strategy of celebrity tie-ins and innovative in-store merchandising environments.
- Increase store traffic and sales during a key sales period.

PROGRAM/STRATEGY

The Get Ready Giveaway was designed to tie into the CBS fall advertising and to accomplish both partners' objectives with a high-visibility program. Key to the strategy was the agreement to leverage CBS's and Kmart's combined marketing, media, and merchandising strengths to minimize expense.

The Get Ready Giveaway, a watch, match, and win game, was the kickoff to consumers. Kmart resolved an otherwise cost prohibitive dilemma of how to get the game cards into millions of households by distributing game information and cards through its 72 million circulars each week for three weeks, a total of 216 million circulars. Each circular included promotional copy for all new shows, a television schedule, and the game card with two separate four-digit numbers. Viewers could play at 8:00 p.m. seven nights a week simply by matching their numbers with the televised spots during all 8:00 p.m. and new prime-time shows. New numbers were telecast each night. To build and maintain momentum, CBS gave Kmart extensive media exposure for the promotion in national and local markets.

Prizes for the game were real "blockbusters." Grand prizes included family dream vacations and Chrysler vans. (Chrysler bartered vans for media.) Third prizes could be redeemed the next day at Kmart, which generated additional store traffic.

Merchandising materials included:
- Get Ready Giveaway signs at Kmart that could be sniped with local TV affiliate call letters.
- Large 3' x 4' banners for stores.
- Prominent cashier banners.
- A continuous loop video showing all new CBS shows in Kmart electronics departments.
- Special Kmart audio tapes promoting CBS shows at 15-minute intervals.
- CBS celebrity guest appearances at Kmart sites.
- "Second-chance" boxes at Kmart stores for depositing game cards.
- Get Ready Giveaway buttons worn by all Kmart employees.
- A Kmart instructional training video produced by CBS and explaining every detail of the promotion.
- A comprehensive instructional manual for Kmart employees.
- A version of the game modified for Kmart employees.
  Support promotion included:
- CBS on-air spots beginning two weeks before the game card dropped.
- A special eight-page insert in *People* magazine.
- A CBS/Kmart electronic press kit.
- A complete package of program materials for all CBS local affiliates.
- Program ads with Get Ready Giveaway mentions in major newspapers and magazines.

RESULTS

According to research by Nielsen, CBS, and Audits and Surveys, the game delivered the following results:

- CBS premiere episode ratings rose 28 percent higher than those of the previous year.
- Awareness was achieved early especially for "Major Dad":
—On the night preceding the game's launch, viewer awareness for "Major Dad" was 39 percent, the highest of any new show in 1989.
—On the following day, when the circular was dropped and the game began, the special preview episode of "Major Dad" awareness jumped to 52 percent.
—Promotion boosted awareness by 33 percent.
- Shows at 8:00 p.m., the specific target of the promotion, were up 20 percent across the board over the previous year's fourth quarter.
- Repeat viewing of new shows was 43 percent, compared to only 37 percent for ABC and NBC.
- Kmart sales increased 6 percent during September.
- Kmart enjoyed a huge increase in readership of the circular.
- The game was played by 1 in every 20 households.
- Heavy TV viewers participated 220 percent more than the general public.
- Combined media value of the promotion was about $24 million, but the investment was a fraction of that amount.
- Roughly 5.5 billion media impressions were generated.

It is interesting to pause here and to consider that virtually any consumer preference or attitude can be influenced by the judicious use of promotion, even TV viewing habits. Promotions are powerful magic.

1989-90

CAMPAIGN/EVENT
Mattel Kids Care Too

COMPANY
Mattel, Inc.

BRAND
Mattel toys

AGENCY
American Consulting Corporation

YEAR
1989-90

BACKGROUND/MARKETING SITUATION

In 1989, Mattel was the second largest toy manufacturer in the United States. The toys category is seasonal, with products selling 60 percent of their total volume at retail during the fourth quarter. Thus competition is very keen within a concentrated time frame. At retail the industry is dominated by large retailers such as Toys 'R' Us, Kmart, and Wal-Mart, the top 10 of these companies controlling more than 50 percent of total toy sales.

Traditionally, the industry books the greater percentage of orders for toys seven to eight months in advance for shipment during the holiday season. Excess inventory after the holidays forces returns to toy manufacturers, deep invoice discounting, and/or very low orders for the following year. Toy companies have two key concerns at this time of year:

- Maintaining existing orders for those products for which there remain manufacturers' production inventory.
- Nurturing sufficient continuous consumer demand to create a clean sell-through of product.

It behooves the manufacturer to differentiate its toy line from the crowd and thereby get the retailer and consumer support necessary to sustain demand.

Help Mattel Help Children

Mattel will donate up to $250,000 in cash and $2 Million in new toys* to charities.

MATTEL CARES

MATTEL KIDS CARE TOO!

OBJECTIVES

With differentiation in mind, the program objectives were clearly defined.

TRADE

- Avoid order cancellations and obtain 4 percent incremental orders on specific products for which manufacturer inventory was expected to exceed sales growth.
- Show higher than industry average sales.
- Gain participation of all of the top 10 retailers.
- Hold post-holiday inventory to no more than 20 percent but no less than 10 percent to avoid out-of-stocks.

CONSUMER

- Generate demand for Mattel products during the peak selling season.
- Maintain brand name awareness throughout the season and create a positive attitude toward key Mattel products.

Success would be measured by the number of events, toys collected, charities participating, major retailers participating, and program awareness as measured by research.

PROGRAM/STRATEGY

Mattel would attempt to appeal to the traditional, benevolent spirit of the season with a program, Mattel Kids Care Too, that would teach children the value of giving. This would give the company a positive image with its buying public and would keep the company's name top-of-mind with consumers during the peak selling season.

Mattel Kids Care Too incorporated toy collection, refurbishing, and distribution. The company tied in with seven national charities and more than 1,000 local not-for-profit organizations. New and used toys were collected at participating retailers, schools, existing and newly created events, and at high-traffic locations. All toys collected, as well as $2 million (retail value) in new Mattel toys and $250,000 in cash were donated to the participating charities for needy children.

Two primary incentives were given to all children and parents who donated a toy: a 4-page product catalog and activity book with either $75 in rebate offers or a $1 instant coupon and a 16-page product catalog and activity book with both $75 in rebates and a $1 instant coupon.

More than 40 million catalogs were distributed at stores, local events, and through magazine inserts. In addition, rebate pads were available at participating retailers for the $75 in rebate offers.

TRADE PROGRAM

Mattel executives presented the program to key customers. They worked with each account to customize its participation in the program. A schedule of events, in addition to retail store events, was created in the top 30 markets for toy collection and distribution. Mattel Kids Care Too kicked off its nationwide program at the Los Angeles Zoo in October 1989. More than 65 celebrities, mainly children, attended the program and donated toys. An additional radio buy was made in the 30 markets to provide supplemental support. Local charities and organizations supported the program with newsletters and fliers.

RESULTS

Mattel Kids Care Too became the most ambitious promotion ever implemented by Mattel and one of its most effective. Key results are summarized below:

Number of Participating Charities	Goal	Actual
National	5	7
Local	30	130
Key Retailer Participation	10	17
Additional Orders vs. Prior Year	25%	33%
Remaining Inventory	20%	14%
Collection Site	80	959
Local Events	9,500	10,156
Activity Book Distribution	41MM	41MM
Toys Collected/Distributed	1,000M	1,386M

The program leveraged a 3.3 times value to buy of radio spots and 139 live remote appearances as well as television mentions. Sales by retailer reflected a direct correlation between the level of participation and sell-through. Mattel Kids Care Too was an overwhelming success because everyone involved cared.

1989-90

CAMPAIGN/EVENT
Eagle Squadron

COMPANY
Eagle Electric Manufacturing Company

BRANDS
Super Spec, Decorator, and SurgeBloc electrical equipment

AGENCY
Don Jagoda Associates

YEAR
1989-90

BACKGROUND/MARKETING SITUATION

In 1989, Eagle Electric Manufacturing Company, a leading manufacturer of electrical switches, wiring devices, and equipment, sold its products nationally, primarily through large electrical supplies distributors who in turn sold to electrical contractors and to individual consumers.

In the electrical supply business, brand identity may be high but loyalty is very low. Eagle's Super Spec, Decorator, and SurgeBloc lines had a reputation for superior quality, but electrical contractors tended to order specific products by type rather than by brand. Eagle had a story to tell during the January-July period, which was the key ordering time for the peak summer construction season, but word-of-mouth was not sufficiently motivating distributors and their counter salespeople.

OBJECTIVES

Eagle's first step was a clear definition of company goals:

- Obtain a degree of brand loyalty in this market during the key six-month purchasing season.
- Increase the number of distributors carrying Eagle products.
- Increase each average purchase of Eagle's Super Spec, Decorator, and SurgeBloc lines.

PROGRAM/STRATEGY

Next was the development of an incentive program with a nostalgic theme that would reinforce brand identity and encourage brand loyalty.

The result was the Eagle Squadron program, a frequent purchase program targeted at distributors and their counter salespeople who directly serve contractors and individual consumers. The program incorporated a military theme based on the famous Eagle Squadron of World War II. It saluted the corporate name and heritage, the company's reputation for "made in America" products, and the fact that many of Eagle's distributors had seen military service. Target audiences were the Eagle sales force, distributors, and distributors' counter salespeople.

The Eagle Squadron encompassed a related incentive program called Write Your Own Ticket, which enabled participants to accumulate program points for Eagle purchases. Points were expressed in "air miles," each of which was equivalent to one mile of air travel on any airline at any time, to any destination in the world or for merchandise in the Write Your Own Ticket catalog. All program materials were designed to recreate the ambiance of the Army Air Corps of World War II:

* All program communications mimicked military correspondence and World War II patriotic posters.
* Distributors "enlisted" in the Eagle Squadron by completing a "recruitment" form for themselves and for their counter salespeople that specified a six-month "tour of duty."
* Distributors submitting their enlistment papers by a March 19 "early bird" date were automatically entered in a sweepstakes awarding a grand prize of two first-class airline tickets to any destination in the United States.
* Following their enlistment, distributors received a sign-up package that included:
—Dog tags for themselves and for their salespeople.
—An Eagle Squadron flight crew cap.
—The Eagle Squadron catalog of merchandise and travel awards, including a special "Quartermaster Store" of military-style merchandise.

Each month distributors received a computerized Mission Briefing statement indicating the value of their purchases in terms of air miles activity. Distributors also received instant-winner scratch-off game cards to award to their counter sales people. Eagle's own sales representatives could also earn air miles points as an override on customer purchases.

RESULTS

Approximately half of all large distributors participated, exceeding Eagle's expectations. Approximately 10 percent of participating distributors were new business clients in Eagle's network. Sales of Eagle featured products increased 33 percent during the promotion — an outstanding result because it came during a recessionary year in the construction industry.

1989-90

CAMPAIGN/EVENT

Sign On, Cash In Game

COMPANY

Prodigy Services Company

BRAND

On-line communication services

YEAR

1989-90

BACKGROUND/MARKETING SITUATION

Prodigy was positioned as the leading information/communication/transactions service within the on-line service industry. Its combination of a low monthly fee and many features afforded Prodigy members access to news, weather, sports, banking, shopping, travel reservations, games, and more. All these services meant Prodigy had a fantastic opportunity for market development, but encouraging members to learn all the features and to use them more frequently was a unique challenge.

OBJECTIVES

The primary objective of this promotion was to increase the number of weekly sessions per member by 20 percent. One secondary objective was to give merchants featured on the service more visibility. Another secondary objective was to turn members' attention to the merchant ads at the bottom of the home computer screen.

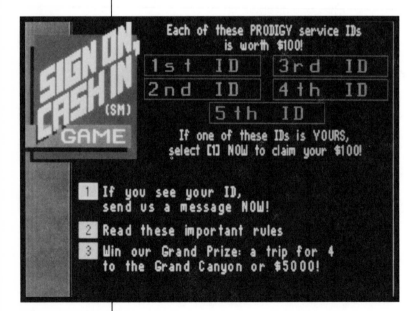

PROGRAM/STRATEGY

Prodigy rose to the challenge with an on-service program that motivated members to use the service every day. Named the Sign On, Cash In Game, its main features were:

- Five randomly drawn member ID's listed daily on the service.
- ID's listed next to ads on a limited number of seeded screens.
- A prize for members who saw their ID's if they sent an acknowledgment electronically.

Daily winners received $100 cash and were automatically entered into a random drawing for the grand prize, a white water rafting trip sponsored by one of the merchants accessible on the service.

Members learned of the promotion by:

- Postcards mailed to their households.
- Representation on the "highlights" screen on the service.
- Ads at the bottom of selected screens.

RESULTS

The results were spectacular:

- A 22 percent increase in weekly sessions per member during Round One (July 17-30).
- A 20 percent increase in weekly sessions per member during Round Two (August 14-27).
- More than half of the members signing on to the service during each week of each round looked for Sign On, Cash In Game ads at the bottom of the screen and followed through to the main screen of the game.

In addition, merchants who received expanded exposure simply by supplying the prizes expressed their satisfaction, although it was not possible to measure their success statistically.

1989-90

CAMPAIGN/EVENT

McDonald's Menu Song

COMPANY

McDonald's Corporation

BRAND

McDonald's full menu

AGENCY

Simon Marketing, Inc.

YEAR

1989-90

BACKGROUND/MARKETING SITUATION

In 1989, McDonald's was the leader in the quick service restaurant category with more than 11,000 restaurants worldwide, estimated total sales of $17.5 billion, and an estimated $1.1 billion spent on advertising and promotion.

An important recent change in the industry had been the move from hamburgers and related offerings to full menu selections. The growth of the nonhamburger items on McDonald's menu, and the communication of those new items to the public, were regarded as critical to continued success. Consequently, McDonald's advertising agency wrote and aired the Menu Song advertising campaign to communicate the wide range of menu choices available at McDonald's throughout the day. It was successful enough that a support promotion seemed logical.

OBJECTIVES

The objectives of the support promotion were:
• Increase sales and transactions.
• Encourage multiple daypart visits.
• Build top-of-mind awareness of menu variety.

PROGRAM/STRATEGY

The plan to mold the Menu Song into an effective consumer promotion used a national solo FSI (76 million circulation; 2,000 newspapers) as its key component.

The FSI contained:

- A 33 rpm record of the Menu Song seeded with one instant million dollar winner at the end of the chorus.
- Six food coupons tailored to individual markets to encourage repeat and dual daypart visits (for example, breakfast and dinner).
- A match-and-win component—consumers could go to McDonald's weekly to redeem coupons and to match a number on the FSI with in-store posted numbers in hopes of winning any of $1.5 million in different prizes.

RESULTS

The results indicated that this innovative event dominated consumer interest as both a promotion vehicle and as an advertising campaign:

- Top-of-mind awareness, as measured by Ad-Watch, was number one nationally.
- Sales projections were exceeded.
- Tremendous national publicity was generated.

The event also deserves special mention because it was the first time a record was dropped in a national FSI and it was the largest one-time pressing of a single record in music history (76 million copies).

1989-90

CAMPAIGN/EVENT

Our Treat

COMPANY

VISA U.S.A. Inc.

BRAND

Credit cards/financial services

AGENCY

Frankel & Co.

YEAR

1989-90

BACKGROUND/MARKETING SITUATION

In the late 1980s, VISA was the leading credit card in the United States. Credit cards were carried by 75 percent of all American consumers, and one out of two adults held a VISA card. Based on this figure, the market was near saturation, and the new battlefront would be convincing consumers to use their cards more often and for larger purchases. During the heavy retail shopping season, October through December, the competition would be concentrating on intense promotional efforts. At the same time, sponsoring banks would be engaging in their own promotional efforts. In addition to this environment, VISA faced a number of internal issues:

- Promotions could not detract or infringe on any member bank's service claim or card enhancement.
- No incentive could be tied to a specific merchant.
- Any promotion had to be open to all VISA card holders regardless of members' willingness to participate.
- A promotion could not require any systems changes by members.

OBJECTIVES

The objectives of the program were:
- Increase card usage by VISA card holders.
- Increase profitability of members' portfolios.
- Acquire 100 percent participation from VISA members.
- Increase VISA payment share at selected test merchants (and hopefully shift share from American Express to VISA).

PROGRAM/STRATEGY

A program was developed that would meet all internal needs of VISA and have universal appeal to consumers.

VISA offered consumers the chance to win a free purchase, whenever and wherever they used their VISA card on randomly selected purchases during a specified period. Winners received award checks equal to the purchase amount. The program was reinforced with the theme line, "VISA, it's everywhere you want to be." During that same time, VISA cardholders could also win a one-of-a-kind VISA millionaire's credit card.

Consumer awareness was created through a :30 "Our Treat" TV commercial, radio and print ads, and point-of-sale materials displayed at merchant test sites.

RESULTS

The results of the program were a treat for VISA, its members, and its consumers:

- From October to December, 1989, VISA sales rose 21 percent.
- Incremental sales of more than $1.4 billion were accrued by VISA.
- Incremental income of nearly $32 million was generated for members.
- There was a 3 to 1 payout of income to expenses for members.
  In addition:
- All 2,000 members participated in the promotion.
- Over $1 million in purchases were awarded.
- Member marketing support exceeded expectations by 300 percent.
- VISA payment share increased from 6.5 percent to roughly 8.5 percent, with American Express share dropping from 6 percent to 5 percent during the promotion.

1989-90

CAMPAIGN/EVENT

Super Bowl XXIII 3-D

COMPANY

Coca-Cola USA

BRAND

Diet Coke

YEAR

1989-90

BACKGROUND/MARKETING SITUATION

Diet Coke was the number-one-selling diet soft drink in the United States. Its marketing plan was aiming to make Diet Coke the number-two-selling soft drink, behind only Coca-Cola Classic. Males were an identified target group for increased volume.

OBJECTIVE

The primary objective of this simple event, in addition to making Diet Coke the number-two-selling soft drink, was to gain incremental Diet Coke sales for January 1989 over January 1988.

PROGRAM/STRATEGY

The strategy was to capitalize on a specific, exclusive marketing opportunity for Diet Coke: SuperBowl XXIII. The focus of the event was the first-ever, live 3-D network television broadcast and commercial for Diet Coke during half-time. Three-D glasses in a corrugated merchandiser were offered to trade accounts in exchange for incremental ads and/or displays for Diet Coke.

RESULTS

An event need not be elaborate to be effective. The results of the 3-D program were the following:

• January case sales rose a remarkable 23 percent.
• The Nielsen share was +14 percent.
• Recall for the campaign slogan was +23 percent.
• $65 million worth of publicity was generated through coverage of the promotion in 2,200 newspapers, on all three television networks and on 850 radio reports.

Incremental displays in high-visibility locations helped stimulate trial and increased sales. The traffic building potential of the 3-D event and "limited supply" of glasses encouraged phenomenal trade support. The "first time" appeal of the event coupled with the exposure on one of the highest viewed sporting events of the year captured consumer enthusiasm and fueled participation.

1989-90

CAMPAIGN/EVENT
Free Pictionary Game

COMPANY
Kraft General Foods Inc.

BRANDS
Kraft Caramels, Kraft Jams, Jellies & Preserves, Kraft Singles, Velveeta Process Cheese

YEAR
1989-90

BACKGROUND/MARKETING SITUATION

The Kraft brands in this promotion were generally used as ingredients for quick meals and snacks. Each of these brands had a strong "kids" franchise, with mom as the gatekeeper. Most of these brands were leaders in their respective categories and had dominant market shares.

In the past, each of the brands had fielded solo promotions targeted to children in the September to February window, the high-volume season. While most promotions were successful, there was an opportunity to generate incremental volume by combining brands for leverage. Kraft hoped to accomplish this end within an event that would offer the trade flexibility in execution.

OBJECTIVES

CONSUMER
- Increase sales 5 percent over the previous year's period.
- Encourage cross-purchase among participating brands.

TRADE
- Expand the promotion window and generate displays in 30 percent ACV during the April/May promotion period.
- Secure A/B feature ads in 30 percent ACV to support the placement of display shippers.

PROGRAM/STRATEGY

Key research findings indicated that mothers like promotions they can receive in-store that have some educational value for their children. The conclusion was to develop an in-store promotion targeted at both mothers and children. The result was the Free Pictionary program.

The Free Pictionary program included the following:

- A major display that appealed to both the retailer and the consumer. Participating retailers received the display filled with 300 Pictionary Special Dinosaur Edition Games, which were free to the consumer with the purchase of any three of the five participating products. The display was supported by display trade funds and a display incentive program. The incentive program offered a second edition Pictionary game to the retailer for building a display with the shipper during the promotion period.

- A point-of-purchase package including display posters and tear pads. The tear pads offered a mini-version of the Pictionary Special Dinosaur Edition Game by mail in the event the store ran out of games.

- Retailers could receive the display package and POS materials directly from the company, thus requiring minimum involvement with the sales force.

The Pictionary Special Dinosaur Edition Game was created expressly for Kraft by Western Publishing, and the display was designed to require minimal floor space, a constant concern of retailers.

RESULTS

The objectives exceeded all quantifiable objectives, particularly noteworthy because this was an off-season event:

- Sales increased 11 percent over the prior year period.
- Display support was 31 percent ACV.
- Feature support reached 59.3 percent with 50.3 percent ACV in A or B features.
- Three million Pictionary Special Dinosaur Edition Games were given to consumers.
- Ten thousand display shippers were placed.
- Twelve thousand second edition full-size Pictionary games were given to the trade as display incentives.

The unique combination of the number-one-selling board game with a dinosaur theme appealed to Moms, kids, and the trade to make this program a success.

1989-90

CAMPAIGN/EVENT

Bank South Kroger Cash Club

COMPANIES

Bank South and Kroger Food Stores

BRANDS

Bank South financial services; Kroger retail grocery

AGENCY

McCann Erickson/Atlanta

YEAR

1989-90

BACKGROUND/MARKETING SITUATION

In the late 1980s, Bank South was the fourth largest bank in Atlanta (second in number of locations), and Kroger was the largest grocery chain in the Atlanta market with a 40 percent share. For two years, Bank South had been waging an aggressive campaign to build a strong consumer franchise in the retail segment of the banking industry.

The Atlanta banking industry was a parity industry with little to distinguish competitive products and services. However, Bank South enjoyed two distinct advantages in this parity market:

- It was the only bank with both free-standing and grocery store locations.
- It was the only bank open seven days a week until 8:00 p.m. — in Kroger stores.

OBJECTIVES

This tie-in promotion would need to serve the goals of both parties:
- Generate account switching from competing banks.
- Open 5,000 new accounts with $10 million in deposits.
- Solidify relationships with existing customers.
- Increase store traffic and convert secondary Kroger shoppers (those using other chains first) to primary Kroger customers.

PROGRAM/STRATEGY

Ideally, the plan would exploit the Bank South/Kroger relationship and add value to being a customer of both. The result was the Bank South/Kroger Cash Club.

Worth 10% more than the money in your pocket.

Bank South Kroger Cash

INTRODUCING BANK SOUTH KROGER CASH

Start saving on your groceries today.

Kroger customers could become members of the club by opening and maintaining any Bank South checking and savings account. Club membership entitled them to save 10 percent on Kroger groceries by purchasing Kroger Cash certificates for 10 percent less than their face value. The program was supported by TV, radio, print, and outdoor to build awareness. The heaviest media was reserved for the end of the week and on weekends, timing that coincided with the busiest shopping periods when all other banks were closed.

RESULTS

The results for Bank South and Kroger were:

- New account openings for Bank South increased 10 percent versus a 1 percent decline for other banks.
- More than 10,000 new accounts were opened to take advantage of Kroger Cash.
- More than 19,000 members participated in the program.
- Bank South Kroger Cash users increased their monthly visits to Kroger by 30 percent.
- Fifty-eight percent of club members shopped at Kroger even when other chains were in a more convenient location.
- Twenty percent of club members became primary Kroger shoppers as a result of the program.

This was such an innovative program and so successful in achieving marketing objectives, that it is an exemplary lesson in forming a tie-in partnership.

1989-90

CAMPAIGN/EVENT

Burger King Kids Club

COMPANY

Burger King Corporation

BRAND

Burger King menu

AGENCY

Alcone Promotion Group

YEAR

1989-90

BACKGROUND/MARKETING SITUATION

Burger King was the second-largest fast food hamburger restaurant chain in the world, with nearly 5,500 restaurants in the United States, 85 percent of which were owned by franchisees. The category has always been intensely competitive, especially in the lucrative youth market (broadly, children under age 12), which was expanding.

Research into the youth market had revealed several important facts:

- Children in this age group are very influential in making the restaurant selection for the entire family.
- Brand loyalty developed at this age influences selection throughout teen and adult years.
- Since the child rarely can come alone, the child's meal generates additional adult transactions.

McDonald's, a competitor, had implemented a major children's program for years. Burger King had not done so consistently and had been suffering a decline in this market since 1984. The need was evident for a strong, turnkey, national youth marketing effort.

OBJECTIVES

Specific objectives of the effort were to:

- Create a program that would influence the restaurant decisions of the entire family.
- Build brand awareness and customer loyalty in children.
- Raise systemwide participation in ongoing children's meal pack and premium programs from 50 percent to 100 percent.
- Create a program attractive enough to other quality national marketers to motivate pooling promotion resources for future youth market events.

PROGRAM/STRATEGY

The Burger King Kids Club was created as a value-added umbrella theme for greater brand recognition.

The program centered on Kids Club characters created by Passion Pictures (developers of Roger Rabbit) to be used in advertising and merchandising. All characters had a contemporary look with special youth interests. In this way, characters communication took on special relevance with kids talking to kids. A series of premiums was developed in conjunction with the Kids Club characters, each featuring a character interacting with a free-wheeling vehicle depicting his/her special interest that actually was a brand and/or product of other high-profile national marketers. Each premium was presented in a Kids Club Meal bag, visible through a unique "premium window," to showcase the premium along with a Kids Club drink cup.

Children could join the club by completing membership application forms at their local Burger King. Support included:

- Complete point-of-sale materials including a counter card with membership application and a merchandising unit describing the program, upcoming premiums and meal offerings, and club sponsor recognition.
- A series of commercials featuring the Kids Club characters.
- A Kids Club membership package sent free to each new member, including a personalized membership card and certificate, letter, stickers, and an autographed picture of a Kids Club character.
- Full-color Kids Club newsletters containing feature stories and ongoing columns "authored" by the characters. These were distributed free in Burger King restaurants to encourage repeat visits.
- Other program elements included character-related headwear giveaways, self-liquidating Kids Club clubhouses, Kids Club birthday party kits and notification program, Kids Club cookies dessert items, local marketing materials, and tie-in promotions with other youth marketers.

A video presentation and brochure introduced the Kids Club program and premium calendar to franchisees. They in turn circulated over 50 million newsletters in the club's first year.

RESULTS

The results were:

- Near-universal participation by franchisees.
- Membership enrollment reaching 10,000 per day, which became the basis for a database to be used for research and direct marketing opportunities.
- Heavier than expected premium orders.
- Tie-in partners who came forth with advertorials and offers in the newsletters.

The Burger King Kids Club was the first nationally executed children's club in the fast food hamburger restaurant industry. It would be followed by others. Imitation is the sincerest form of flattery.

1990-1991

REGGIE

AWARDS

CAMPAIGNS

OLYMPIC FESTIVAL '90 PIN PROMOTION — RAINBOW FOODS

THE DOUGHBOY'S 25TH BIRTHDAY — THE PILLSBURY COMPANY

KRAFT SINGLES OUTRAGEOUS SANDWICH CONTEST — KRAFT GENERAL FOODS INC.

MAGICUP INSTANT-WIN GAME — COCA-COLA COMPANY — FOUNTAIN DIVISION

A SHOT AT TAKING STOCK IN THE CELTICS — MILLER BREWING COMPANY

HALFWAY CHALLENGE — THE GILLETTE COMPANY

FREE TOOTHBRUSH TIE-IN — COLGATE PALMOLIVE COMPANY AND WARNER-LAMBERT INC.

TEENAGE MUTANT NINJA TURTLES — PIZZA HUT, INC.

TOUCH & GO — MONSANTO LAWN & GARDEN

1990 NINTENDO WORLD CHAMPIONSHIPS — NINTENDO

1990-91

CAMPAIGN/EVENT

Olympic Festival '90 Pin Promotion

COMPANY

Rainbow Foods

AGENCY

McCracken Brooks Communications, Inc.

YEAR

1990-91/Super Reggie

BACKGROUND/MARKETING SITUATION

At the time of this promotion, Rainbow Foods was the leading grocer in the Minneapolis/St. Paul area. With a 24 percent share of market, it was just ahead of Cub Foods, the original super warehouse grocer in the Twin Cities area. Rainbow's success came from its willingness to use aggressive promotional tactics in innovative ways.

OBJECTIVES

The objectives related to Rainbow's U.S. Olympic Festival '90 sponsorship and focused on the need to:

- Differentiate Rainbow from its competitors.
- Increase traffic and sales in all 22 stores.
- Maximize the impact of sponsorship.
- Offset sponsorship costs.

PROGRAM/STRATEGY

Research had indicated that pin trading enjoyed international popularity. The Rainbow Olympic Festival Pin Promotion made Rainbow the first sponsor in Olympic history to use this kind of program as an overlay. The strategy developed would set Rainbow apart not only from its business competitors, but also from other Olympic sponsors.

For a six-month period, each Rainbow store became official Pin

Headquarters for the U.S. Olympic Festival '90 pictogram pins. Forty-seven pins were designed, featuring 37 sports, plus 10 others showing unique aspects of the Olympic Festival.

To elicit regional support and to help offset expenses, Rainbow offered local food brokers and national packaged goods manufacturers pins assigned to their products in return for a $25,000 participation fee. These tie-ins gave pin sponsors radio endorsements, eight weeks of feature ads and displays, dedicated point-of-sale in-store, and lots of consumer good-will.

The promotion was supported by a turnkey campaign:

- Twenty-four weeks of radio and newspaper advertising.
- In-store point-of-sale materials.
- Weekly fliers.
- Major display activity for participating partner products.
- Educational pin-trading brochure for consumers.
- Eight weeks of feature ads and displays in all Rainbow stores.
- Pins offered for 49¢ with purchase of partner products or $3.99 without purchase. Each pin was available for a limited time.

RESULTS

This was Rainbow's largest promotion ever, with 47 participating brands providing more than $1 million in promotion funds for the program. The program built continuity with repeat purchases to get the entire set of pins. Consumers were tenacious in their return visits to stores and assiduous in purchasing the correct products for each pin. Rainbow moved more than 1 million pins.

All promotional costs, including the $300,000 sponsorship fee, were self-liquidated. There was a 5 to 10 percent increase in overall sales volume and a 15 to 20 percent increase in sales volume for participating brands.

1990-91

CAMPAIGN/EVENT
The Doughboy's 25th Birthday

COMPANY
The Pillsbury Company

BRANDS
Pillsbury flour, cake mixes, rolls, cookies, frosting, and Hungry Jack biscuits

AGENCIES
Leo Burnett Company; Amrein Marketing Associates; Ultra Creative

YEAR
1990-91

BACKGROUND/MARKETING SITUATION

Pillsbury was the leading company in branded baked goods in both the shelf-stable bakery mixes/flour and the refrigerated dough categories. A major challenge for players in this area is gaining and maintaining retailer support. In the shelf-stable category, in particular, competition for limited space makes incremental volume and share very difficult to achieve. This situation calls for promotions that cut through the clutter to capture consumer interest. Pillsbury found its "clutter cutter" in 1990 with the Pillsbury Doughboy's 25th birthday. According to Q-scores, the Doughboy was America's number one brand character.

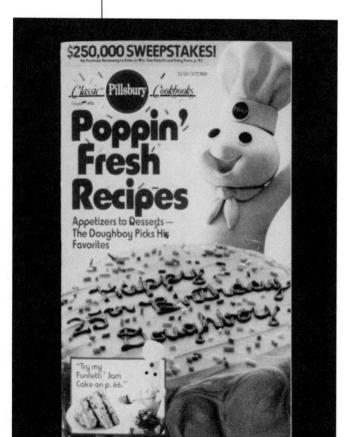

OBJECTIVES

Pillsbury wished to celebrate the Doughboy's 25th birthday for several purposes:
- To generate awareness for all brands.
- To deliver incremental volume across participating brands.
- To leverage the Pillsbury name in a way that would be more effective and efficient than multiple solo events.
- To provide merchandising opportunities for the sales force.

PROGRAM/STRATEGY

The strategy eventually chosen would leverage both the Doughboy and Pillsbury's "critical mass" of products with the trade. This strategy selected Sears as a tie-in partner to generate strong secondary awareness. The turnkey program, the Doughboy's 25th Birthday Party, encompassed a creative mixture of marketing elements that were mutually supportive.

It was the first time that Pillsbury used TV network advertising for a promotion. In the commercial, the Doughboy blew out candles on his cake, then directed consumers to grocery stores and Sears outlets to pick up entry forms for the Doughboy Trivia Sweepstakes. Prizes for the sweepstakes were a $25,000 Sears kitchen makeover, ranges, and microwave ovens. Correct answers to the trivia questions were printed on point-of-sale materials.

Trade support activities were planned to inspire retailers to participate fully. A teaser mailing distributed limited edition Doughboy dolls and in-store birthday videos. A grocery retail display contest awarded winners a limited edition Doughboy gumball machine. To focus attention on the promotion, retailers could also arrange for Doughboy guest appearances and commemorative pins.

Consumers got product coupons and a Doughboy doll premium offer delivered via FSI and Classic Cookbook magazine.

Public relations electronic and print campaigns rounded out the celebration.

RESULTS

The following were the results:

- The PR program generated 700 print, 850 radio, and 140 broadcast television stories about the Doughboy's birthday, totalling more than 225 million audience exposures with a value of nearly $500,000.
- Total consumer purchases increased across all brands, with some brands up as much as nearly 25 percent.
- Merchandising support increased on all key variables (feature and display).
- More than 100,000 consumers sent for the Doughboy doll and millions redeemed free product coupons.

Not to mention hundreds of birthday greetings. This was the Pillsbury Doughboy's happiest birthday ever.

1990-91

CAMPAIGN/EVENT

Kraft Singles Outrageous Sandwich Contest

COMPANY

Kraft General Foods Inc.

BRANDS

Kraft Singles, Kraft Miracle Whip, Kraft Mayonnaise

YEAR

1990-91

BACKGROUND/MARKETING SITUATION

As of 1990, Kraft Singles led the process cheese category with a 41.0 share. Singles was purchased mainly by women 25 to 54 years old with children 6 to 12 years old in the household. The primary food preparation use was for sandwiches.

The category has always been characterized by lack of consumer loyalty, and Singles had been experiencing a decline in market share, mostly due to increased competition from a rival national brand and private label imitators. However, there was still opportunity to expand usage. Kraft research had revealed that of all sandwiches consumed, 74 percent are cheese compatible but only 22 percent actually include a piece of cheese.

OBJECTIVES

Kraft needed to increase incremental take-away. To do so, they would have to encourage the target audience, mothers and children, to make more sandwiches and motivate the trade to build secondary displays of Singles with sandwich-related items.

PROGRAM/STRATEGY

Kraft organized a recipe contest for children that would involve mothers and would communicate to the trade a promise of profits through the sale of related items.

The Kraft Singles Outrageous Sandwich Contest inspired creative sandwich use among kids by offering a free bread coupon with the purchase of Kraft products for sandwiches. The contest included sales force, trade, and consumer elements with a broad publicity overlay.

The Outrageous Sandwich Contest was open to kids 6 to 14 years old, with the 6- to 10-year-old group being judged separately from the 11 to 14 year olds. There were 10 grand prizes (five for each level):

- All-expense paid trip to Walt Disney World Resort for four days.
- Participation in the final judging and awards ceremony to determine the most outrageous sandwich.

To qualify for entry, a sandwich had to contain at least one slice of Kraft Singles combined with any other edible ingredients. Kids named their sandwich creations and sent the recipes to contest headquarters. Recipes were judged by distinguished food editors as well as by the head chef of Walt Disney World. A special honorary judge was none other than Mickey Mouse, the biggest cheese fan of all.

Press kits were first sent to 500 major newspapers and to leading women's magazines. A full-page national FSI announcing the contest and the free bread offer dropped in early April. One week later a one-third-page Sunday Comics ad again solicited entries. May issues of Disney Channel magazine repeated the contest announcement. Stores were provided with posters which carried tear-off entry forms.

RESULTS

Thousands of recipes were received from children all over the country. All states were represented. Many individual stores and chains held their own minicontests. Some built enormous displays of Kraft Singles and sandwich fixings and supported their events with co-op radio. The 10 winners prepared their sandwiches at a special ceremony at Disney World.

There was an incremental volume increase of 2.3 million pounds, 21 percent over the base. The contest generated 100,000 pounds more volume than the prior most successful event for Singles. PromotionScan reported that this was due totally to merchandising support. The percent ACV feature and display activity in some areas more than doubled the promotion norm. The contest was picked up by many daily newspapers, supplementing the FSI and Sunday Comics circulation by 10 million. The finals were broadcast on local Orlando news and hometown papers carried feature stories on the winners.

1990-91

CAMPAIGN/EVENT

Magicup Instant-Win Game

COMPANY

Coca-Cola Company — Fountain Division

YEAR

1990-91

BACKGROUND/MARKETING SITUATION

Coca-Cola Fountain, an operating unit of The Coca-Cola Company, was the leading supplier of fountain beverages to the United States foodservice industry. It sold Coca-Cola classic, Diet Coke, and Sprite, all of which were number-one brands in their categories. Primary channels included fast food and convenience stores; regional chain and independent restaurants; theaters, stadiums, and arenas; contract feeders; and cup vending.

By the mid-1980s, the dramatic growth in the number of foodservice outlets experienced in the previous decade had gone flat. Because soft drinks were the most profitable items on a food service menu, they became even more important for profitability. Early "on-the-cup" games had been successful as traffic and sales builders, but they presented several obstacles:

- Medium-sized chains could only afford generic games on stock cups with stock prizes.
- Small chains often could not afford to participate at all.
- "Everyone wins" games had the greatest appeal, but few outlets could afford the funding.
- Most games were designed only for fast food or convenience stores. They were not relevant to other channels.

OBJECTIVES

Coca-Cola's Fountain Division sought to circumvent the drawbacks to on-the-cup games. With new cup technology, they could hope to achieve both consumer and trade objectives.

CONSUMER

- Increase total soft drink incidence.
- Increase total ounces per serving.

VENDORS

- Increase total soft drink buying rate (incidence x ounces) and profit per participating outlet.

- Achieve total participation of 25,000 outlets.
- Sell in 100 million promotional cups of soft drink.

PROGRAM/STRATEGY

Coca-Cola estimated that by adding value to a soft drink purchase, volume and frequency of purchases would increase. Through a proprietary new software program, the Magicup instant-win game was the first on-the-cup label game with an "everyone wins" format to be executed as a single national game with over 300 custom executions.

Unlike previous costly on-the-cup programs, whereby expensive game cups with pre-attached instant-win labels were distributed, Magicup was simply a pre-seeded label designed to affix to the retailer's own cups. Retailers participating at the 100,000 label level were able to seed in their own custom food discount prize or one preselected channel offer prize into the bank of prizes provided by Coca-Cola without disturbing the integrity of the national game rules. This feature provided a degree of ownership many mid-sized and smaller chains could not find in earlier on-the-cup programs. More than 132 million labels, primarily for use on 32-ounce or larger cups, were produced for 300 different offer variations, customized for each of the participating chains and outlets. Smaller retailers received Magicup labels pre-affixed to Coca-Cola trademark cups. Thus, maximum opportunity for participation was assured.

Specific promotional support included:

- Custom point-of-sale counter cards with the vendor's own offer included as a snipe on the display.
- Television commercials featuring the New Kids on the Block.

RESULTS

CONSUMER

- Sixty-six percent trial among those aware of Magicup.
- More than 80 percent same-month repeat Magicup purchase.
- Twenty-five percent of consumers said Magicup influenced them to purchase a soft drink they would not otherwise have purchased (increased incidence).
- Thirty-five percent said Magicup encouraged them to buy a larger-than-usual size soft drink (increase ounces).

TRADE

- Participation by 52,000 outlets.
- More than 12 percent volume increase in fast food chains.
- More than 146 percent increase vs. prior year in convenience stores.
- More than 13 percent volume increase in family restaurants.
- More than 17 percent volume increase in leisure outlets.
- A 13% increase in trade-up to 44 oz.
- Nine percent increase on 32-ounce size at theaters.
- Vendor participation was greater than for any previous Coca-Cola Fountain national promotion ever.

1990-91

CAMPAIGN/EVENT

A Shot at Taking Stock in the Celtics

COMPANY

Miller Brewing Company

BRAND

Miller Genuine Draft

YEAR

1990-91

BACKGROUND/MARKETING SITUATION

From the time of its introduction in 1986, Miller Genuine Draft had grown to be ninth in beer sales in the United States, the fastest growing beer. Competition in the premium segment of the beer industry was intense, and Genuine Draft's growth in the Boston market was behind the brand's growth in the rest of the country. Boston's seven independent distributors carried a full line of competing products as well as Miller brands. Local promotions had been proven to be most effective in moving large volumes of beer in the target market, men ages 21 to 25.

OBJECTIVES

The overall objective was to increase the brand's growth in the Boston area. Boston-area distributors were given these specific objectives:

- Exceed the monthly sales task goal.
- Obtain free-standing displays in the top 20 percent of off-premise accounts (retailers).
- Conduct an in-house incentive.

PROGRAM/STRATEGY

The strategy was to get the attention of distributors with a retail program combining three elements: Boston Celtics, Celtics stock, and comedian Dennis Miller. One of the NBA's greatest teams, the Boston Celtics are also unique because they are one of only two professional sports franchises that sell their stock to the public. Genuine Draft was the malt beer sponsor of the NBA and a

telecast sponsor of the Celtics, while Miller had just hired Dennis Miller as spokesperson.

A kick-off luncheon for distributors and 70 retailers featured Dennis Miller shooting a TV commercial for the promotion, A Shot at Taking Stock in the Celtics. A total of 29 consumers could each instantly win 100 shares of Celtics stock seeded inside packages of Genuine Draft. A second-chance mail-in was also available, and local radio stations offered the chance to be one of five winners.

The commercial ran on all Celtics telecasts and on the local CBS NBA Game of the Week. It also was supported by :15 and :30 promotional spots. Radio station WBCN ran 100 recorded promotional spots in addition to giving away the shares of Celtics stock on Thursday mornings. All promotional spots drove consumers to retail for a chance to win shares.

The promotion was supported at retail with:
- Dennis Miller 5' free-standing cutouts.
- Display card with entry forms.
- Case card with entry forms.
- Package stickers.
- 3' x 4' banners.
- "Shareholders" (can coolers).

Distributors received an introductory videotape for use at sales meetings.

RESULTS

The sales display execution and excitement generated positioned Genuine Draft as a growing force in the Boston market:
- Sales increased 100 percent over 1989; a double-digit increase in May was also recorded.
- Display was obtained in 89 percent of accounts. Goal had been 20 percent.
- For April, Miller led with 42 ad features, compared to 40 for Coors and 16 for Budweiser.
- The promotion began a successful trend in sales throughout the 1990 year.

1990-91

CAMPAIGN/EVENT
Halfway Challenge
COMPANY
The Gillette Company
BRAND
Right Guard
AGENCY
Phone Works
YEAR
1990-91

BACKGROUND/MARKETING SITUATION

In the late 1980s, Right Guard deodorant for men had sought to break away from its competition with a high-profile sports image that included sponsorships with major sports in conjunction with sports-oriented advertising and packaging. Gillette's sponsorship of the NASCAR auto racing series was meant to be an important part of that strategy, but initial results were disappointing. Many TV viewers were unaware that Right Guard was offering a $10,000 prize to the driver in the lead at the halfway mark. They tuned in for the end of the race only.

OBJECTIVES

Gillette needed a better way to leverage the NASCAR sponsorship, specifically to:
• Raise sales of Right Guard in target markets.
• Obtain in-store display and feature advertising in NASCAR markets (South and West).
• Increase participation and viewership by males, ages 18–35, of NASCAR televised races.

PROGRAM/STRATEGY

The strategy was to develop a promotion that would reward participants for watching NASCAR events in the Right Guard Halfway Challenge. TV viewers were encouraged to call a 900 number before the halfway point in each race, which would register them for a chance to win a grand prize—a Pontiac Grand Prix SE— by punching in their telephone numbers. Then randomly selected outbound calls were made to the registrants, who would qualify for the drawing by naming the leader at the halfway point in the race. The grand prize winner was announced before the end of the race. Once a winner was confirmed, the name was transferred to ESPN for broadcast announcement.

Media included:

- National and local advertising in newspapers and on TV announcing the 900 number.
- Point-of-sale tear-off entry forms and write-in materials.
- ESPN broadcast of the 900 number throughout the first half of the race.

RESULTS

NASCAR drivers, consumers, Right Guard sales force, and retailers enthusiastically supported this event:

- NASCAR directors called the promotion "the largest in NASCAR history."
- Editorial space was picked up in *USA Today* and in other national publications.
- More than 1 million entries were received throughout the program.
- The 900 number received free announcements on national TV during 8 of the 14 live races and during all 14 races on national radio, including announcement of the winning consumer at the end of each race.
- Gillette received its highest display support ever in most markets and reported up to triple-digit share increases in markets where the promotion ran.
- The company gathered a significant database for a follow-up campaign.

With its success in an uncharted territory, the Right Guard Halfway Challenge inspired other marketers to use 900 numbers in their own future events.

1990-91

CAMPAIGN/EVENT
Free Toothbrush Tie-In

COMPANIES
Colgate Palmolive Company and Warner-Lambert Inc.

BRANDS
Colgate toothpaste, Colgate PLUS toothbrushes, Listerine and Listermint mouthwashes

AGENCY
Langworth Taylor Company, Inc.

YEAR
1990-91

BACKGROUND/MARKETING SITUATION

The brands participating in this promotion competed in the dental health market, which included the following segments:

- Dentifrice: the largest segment, dominated in the United States by Crest (number one) and Colgate (number two) and worldwide by Colgate (number one).
- Mouthwash: led in the United States by Listerine and Listermint in the fluoride segment; the cosmetic segment leader was Scope.
- Toothbrushes: dominated in the United States by Colgate (number one); major players included Reach (Johnson & Johnson) and Oral B.

The key to continued dominance was display, which was becoming more difficult to increase due to the expanding number of brands competing for a limited amount of shelf and display space.

OBJECTIVES

The objectives of the program were the following:

- Increase incremental consumer take-away.
- Achieve the highest level of trade support in the history of the brands.
- Enlarge the Black and Hispanic franchises.

PROGRAM/STRATEGY

Colgate and Warner-Lambert planned to leverage the strengths of their combined

brands in an event so exciting that it would encourage the trade to participate with record levels of display.

To encourage trade display, prebuilt mini-pallets were developed. All trade accounts were surveyed in advance and the pallets built to their requirements. Pallets contained Listerine, Listermint, and a variety of Colgate toothbrushes. The pallets functioned as a free standing end aisle display and carried tear pads with a mail-in version of the free toothbrush offer.

The program had the following components and overlays:

- An FSI coupon with instant gratification for a free Colgate PLUS toothbrush with purchase of one Colgate toothpaste and one Listerine or Listermint mouthwash.
- Joint sales presentations by the sales forces of both companies.
- A dental health message conveyed by the slogan "For a Clean and Healthy Mouth."
- A TV campaign featuring all products and the free toothbrush offer in a :15 spot, with most frequent airing a week before the FSI.
- A special bilingual sell sheet and point-of-sale materials developed for ethnic markets.

RESULTS

The highest level of display in the history of Colgate Toothpaste was generated, with near-record national shares. Display and feature each exceeded the best prior events by 10 and 25 percent respectively. Contributing to this success was the combined efforts of two competing companies who joined forces to develop a record number of multibrand, prebuilt pallets.

1990-91

CAMPAIGN/EVENT

Teenage Mutant Ninja Turtles

COMPANY

Pizza Hut, Inc.

AGENCY

The Ryan Partnership

YEAR

1990-91

BACKGROUND/MARKETING SITUATION

As the world's largest pizza chain, Pizza Hut was the national market share leader in carry-out sales. To maintain its strong market position, Pizza Hut needed new promotional opportunities to combat increasing competition from every kind of QSR (quick service restaurant). Because children influence 83 percent of all QSR family dining decisions, it was critical for Pizza Hut to build its image and loyalty in the "kids market."

OBJECTIVES

The objectives of the program were to:

- Build image, appeal, loyalty, and long-term sales among kids and their families.
- Increase Pizza Hut system sales during a traditionally slow period, the month of September.

PROGRAM/STRATEGY

The chain intended to drive family traffic to Pizza Hut with a self-liquidating premium offer featuring America's hottest kids-oriented entertainment property, the Teenage Mutant Ninja Turtles. The target was kids, ages 6–12, skewing slightly toward boys, and the fit was perfect because every child knew that pizza was the Turtles' favorite food.

Pizza Hut secured the exclusive rights to feature the Turtles as recording artists and as a rock music group in live performance. The program included the following:

- Audiocassette: Ten "original" songs, available only through Pizza Hut, performed by the "actual" Turtles. This sold for $3.99 with any pizza purchase ($10 value).
- Free four-color Activity Booklet with pull-out autographed poster included in the offer.
- Coming Out of Their Shells concert tour staged in top 40 markets.
- Interactive show featuring songs from the audiocassette.
- Public relations and local store marketing incorporating store visits by the Turtles, ticket giveaways, and ideas for media stretch.
- Co-sponsorship of Nickelodeon's third annual Nick Takes over Your School sweepstakes, which featured a guest appearance by the Turtles at the winner's school.
- Radio and TV commercial support for Pizza Hut restaurants in local markets.
- Print support: FSI, direct mail, door hangers, on-pack offers, in-store pole hangers, posters, table tents, counter cards, and more.
- Radio cross-promotions like Fresh from the Sewers, a contest seeking the most original Turtle "lingo" line.
- Pay-per-view cable tie-in: live telecast of the Turtles concert from Radio City Music Hall. During September, 200 pay-per-view cable commercials advertised the offer for the audiocassette and a tour guide. These free :30 spots reached 40 million homes. In return, pay-per-view ads were inserted into the polybags containing the audiocassettes, and pay-per-view stickers were affixed to the audiocassettes and to each Turtles floor display.
- Live Home Video Release tie-in: Pizza Hut negotiated the rights to the videocassette version of the Turtles movie. Pizza Hut received placement of a :60 commercial on the front of 7 million videos, prominent exposure on Live Home Video's TV, radio, and print advertising, point-of-sale mentions, and the right to place a coupon book in each video.
- Video poster giveaway with purchase.
- Tie-in with Konami for developing a Turtles home video game. Pizza Hut placed 3 million coupons for free personal pan pizzas into the packages and ran a national sweepstakes with various video games as prizes.

RESULTS

Pizza Hut was extremely successful in linking the hottest kids' property with its product:

- The Turtles' debut album was an unprecedented double platinum phenomenon—2 million copies were sold through the 6,000 Pizza Hut restaurants.
- This was the first time an audiocassette was marketed exclusively through a chain of restaurants.
- Attendance at Pizza Hut was well above all past records and above projections.
- The communications effort resulted in near-total saturation of the market. Pizza Hut had become the de facto headquarters of the Teenage Mutant Ninja Turtles.

1990-91

CAMPAIGN/EVENT
Touch & Go
COMPANY
Monsanto Lawn & Garden
BRANDS
Roundup and Greensweep
AGENCY
The Patrick Company
YEAR
1990-91

BACKGROUND/MARKETING SITUATION

Monsanto Lawn & Garden manufactured two leading consumer lawn and garden chemical product lines: Roundup, an environmentally safe weed killer; and Greensweep, a full line of pre-mixed liquid hose-end sprays for lawns. Each had a commanding market share in its category. The lawn chemicals industry is heavily regulated by the Environmental Protection Agency, with increased attention being given to educating the trade as well as the consumer.

Roundup and Greensweep were sold through distributors and then to various classes of retail trade, including nurseries, independent hardware stores, home building centers, and some grocery outlets where they were positioned in a confusing and inconsistent environment on the shelf. Technical and seasonal product information was essential to help bewildered customers make purchase decisions. Thus, training the retail floor salesperson to be an authority on Monsanto lawn and garden chemicals was considered critical to sales success, especially because Monsanto had to defend its share against competitors like Ortho.

OBJECTIVES

The purpose of the promotion was to familiarize retail store personnel with basic product knowledge. The following were the objectives of the program:
- Develop training for the retail salesperson that would be fun, instructive, and informative.
- Gain maximum store participation out of a universe of 30,000 outlets.
- Get permission from store managers to distribute program materials to store personnel.

PROGRAM/STRATEGY

The strategy was to create an easy-to-play game in a paperless format that would reward incentives to managers for signing up on the program and to salespeople for correct answers to product information questions. The program developed to this end was an 800 number telephone call-in game named Touch & Go.

Participants were allowed to call up to three times a week to take a variety of quizzes about Monsanto products. The program worked this way:
- A full complement of educational materials and a back-room poster made the game easy to understand.
- Callers were asked random true/false product-related questions from a series of 30 questions. Responses could be made by using a touch-tone phone.
- Correct responses could be turned into instant-win merchandise prizes and entry into a sweepstakes for travel prizes.
- An incorrect answer triggered immediate training over the phone.
- The game was designed by AT&T to continue for eight weeks with weekly participation counts relayed to Monsanto.

RESULTS

Program results showed that Touch & Go was top-of-mind with those who sold Monsanto products:
- Roundup and Greensweep enjoyed a 23 percent increase in sales over the previous year.
- On an average, three salespersons per outlet participated.
- There was an average correct response rate of 93 percent, which meant that knowledge was reinforced and validated.
- Approximately 62 percent of participants tried to play more than the maximum three times per week allowed.
- Salespersons increased displaying Monsanto consumer materials on shelf.

1990-91

CAMPAIGN/EVENT

1990 Nintendo World Championships

COMPANIES

Primary: Nintendo

Secondary: Kraft/General Foods, Thomas J. Lipton Company, Nabisco,
Pepsi Cola Company, Reebok International, Ltd.

BRANDS

Chips Ahoy! cookies (Nabisco), Jell-O Pudding and Gelatin Pops (Kraft), Nintendo hardware
and software, Nintendo Real Fruit Snacks (Lipton), Pepsi Cola, Reebok athletic footwear

AGENCY

Entertainment Marketing Communications International

YEAR

1990-91

BACKGROUND/MARKETING SITUATION

Video games are a well established entertainment medium with all ages of mainstream Americans, especially younger people. Nintendo video hardware and characters were first in popularity in 1990, enjoying an 80 percent market share. Nintendo's two main competitors, Sega and Atari, were in aggressive pursuit with technological advances.

Nintendo realized it needed a turn-key event that would be a definitive statement of its market dominance. Looking to other market leaders with similar demographics, Nintendo tied in with Kraft/General Foods, Lipton, Nabisco, Pepsi Cola, and Reebok to develop a mega-event.

OBJECTIVES

The objectives for Nintendo were to:

- Stimulate demand for the entire Nintendo franchise.
- Introduce new users to the category.
- Introduce hot new games coming soon to retail.

- Create strong visibility for Nintendo during off-peak sales periods.
  The objectives for secondary sponsors were to:
- Increase brand awareness through multimedia exposures.
- Increase market share.
- Strengthen each brand's identity as a preferred product choice for active, adventurous young people on the cutting edge of social trends.

PROGRAM/STRATEGY

Nintendo elected to create the ultimate challenge for players from novice to master levels of competition—the Nintendo World Championships (NWC)—a tour in 30 markets across the country from March through December 1990. The 75,000-square-foot production drew more than 600,000 players and fans and culminated at a championship playoff at Universal Studios in Los Angeles. Tickets were sold at major ticket outlets, on-site, and by advance mail.

TRADE

Nintendo trade promotion served as the superstructure for NWC, with each secondary partner implementing its own related events. Nintendo activity included:

- Coverage by every leading radio and TV station for each city.
- Two full-page ads in leading newspapers two weeks prior to NWC in each city.
- A $100,000 budget for radio, TV, and print given to a local promoter in each market.
- Advertorial inserts or sections in certain key markets.

One activity popular with local retailers was a $2 discount off the price of general admission, distributed in the retailer's name, in return for airtime, circulars, or ticket distribution. There were also Nintendo Gameboy giveaways and various sweepstakes for Nintendo prizes, all supplied by Nintendo.

CONSUMER

Consumer promotion was primed with media support from secondary sponsors. Reebok ran :05 NWC tags on its commercials, 30 black and white newspaper ads, and 30 color ads in the Sunday comics offering a chance to win a free trip to the finals. Jell-O tagged TV ads and ran 40 million FSIs announcing its "game tips" on-pack promotion in addition to 30 ads for a buy-one/get-one-free ticket promotion. Lipton also ran 30 ads but offered a coupon to make a free music video at NWC.

Nintendo gave away free program books at NWC and supported NWC with Nintendo Power magazine ads. Nintendo mailed flyers to all subscribers with an 800 number for TicketMaster outlets. A 900 number for the NWC schedule hotline ran on Nabisco cookies and Jell-O pops packages. Nintendo also sent Super Mario Brothers characters to tour malls and distributed Mario Bucks ($10 discounts on Nintendo products) to NWC semifinalists.

Reebok placed 3,500 displays containing Nintendo Power magazines featuring a scratch-and-win Nintendo game free with a $30 Reebok purchase.

Lipton manned a "make your own video" booth on the NWC show floor. Consumers could dance to rap music with the Fruit Snacks theme and take their video home free for two proofs-of-purchase plus the FSI coupon or for $6 cash.

Oreo and Chips Ahoy! in-packed 15,000 NWC tickets in a scratch-and-win program on 2 million packages.

Pepsi gave away $2 NWC discount coupons at retail and implemented Nintendo Gameboy giveaways via take-one pads.

RESULTS

The following were the results:

- Nintendo market share increased to 90 percent, and its first-half 1990 sales for Nintendo Entertainment Systems and Gameboys were 30 percent higher than the previous year's.
- Nintendo's total free media impressions from barter and publicity topped 551 million.
- Nintendo's 900 number hotline received 10,000 calls per month.
- A related incentive sales/trade program for Jell-O received more than 300 responses from food brokers and food chains.
- Lipton sampled more than 450,000 fruit snacks and distributed more than 150,000 cents-off coupons.
- Pepsi was the only beverage served in 75 percent of the buildings in the NWC; 25 percent switched from Coke specifically for the NWC promotion.
- Pepsi enjoyed incremental end-aisle displays in 70 percent of the NWC markets.
- Virtually all Reebok free sneaker gift certificates were redeemed.

1991-1992

REGGIE

AWARDS

CAMPAIGNS

SOUND OFF PROMOTION — THE SOUTHLAND CORPORATION

THE LITTLE ENGINE THAT COULD — SHOPKO STORES, INC.

FREE RIDE PROMOTION — WESTERN UNION FINANCIAL SERVICES INC.

HARVEST OF GOOD FOODS — CAMPBELL SOUP COMPANY/CSC ADVERTISING

1991 EASTER OPEN HOUSE/PHOTOS WITH THE
CRAYOLA BUNNY — HALLMARK CARDS, INC.

DRIVE CLEANER—WIN A BEAMER — SUPERAMERICA GROUP, INC., AND ASHLAND OIL COMPANY

TENTH ANNIVERSARY SWEEPSTAKES — THE NUTRASWEET COMPANY

MAALOX MOMENTS RADIO CAMPAIGN — RHONE-POULENC RORER

TEAM SPIRIT PROGRAM — LEAF, INC.

GENERAL HOSPITAL REINTRODUCTION — AMERICAN BROADCASTING COMPANY

1991-92

CAMPAIGN/EVENT
Sound Off

COMPANY
The Southland Corporation

BRAND
Convenience store shopping

AGENCIES
Promotional Resources Group, Inc. and W.B. Donner

YEAR/AWARD
1991-92/Super Reggie

BACKGROUND/MARKETING SITUATION

With 6,500 7-Eleven stores in North America, Southland Corporation was the world's largest convenience retailer. Each store served around 1,100 customers per day.

7-Eleven sold over 1 million cups of fresh-brewed coffee per day, making it the largest seller of take-out/off-premise coffee in the country. The chain also sold approximately 25 million fountain drinks per month, making it one of the largest sellers of fountain soft drinks in the country. However, unlike most of its competitors, 7-Eleven offered a full range of drinks, including Coca-Cola, Pepsi, Dr Pepper, and Mountain Dew.

7-Eleven's heavy coffee and fountain drink consumers already accounted for a significant proportion of the chain's coffee and soft drink sales. However, unit sales were flat, and a series of price-offs had started to erode the perceived retail value of the products.

OBJECTIVES

Southland sought a way to drive medium users to 7-Eleven more frequently to co-opt a

larger share of their coffee and fountain drink purchases. These were the objectives for the program:

- Increase coffee and fountain soft drink volume by three percent in February and March.
- Raise overall sales above projected trends with no margin decrease (no discounting/price-offs).
- Extend the dollar of existing media buys by 25 percent.
- Develop a low-cost promotion with little or no increase above normal expenditures for media and point-of-purchase materials.

PROGRAM/STRATEGY

Two consumer motivations were considered in development of the strategy:
- People want to be part of "history in the making."
- People want their opinions to count, and they'll even pay to hear the results of an opinion poll if they have participated.

Thus, Sound Off was born. Every week a question of local or national interest was communicated to the general public via radio with in-store support. People could vote their opinion on the subject by going to a 7-Eleven store and buying a fountain soft drink or coffee in a cup marked "Yes" or "No." Regular nonpromotion cups were made available for undecided voters. Customers who wanted to vote but did not purchase a drink could cast their vote on an in-store entry form. Customers could "sound off" as many times as they wished by returning to any 7-Eleven store.

The Sound Off question of the week was broadcast via radio each Monday morning and posted at several in-store locations. The following is a sample of the kinds of national questions asked:
- Do you think men are better drivers than women?
- If an ATM made an error and gave you several hundred dollars too much, would you return the money?
- Did you learn the facts of life from your parents?
    Several divisions expressed interest in local issues. A few from the New York area were:
- If Donald Trump ran for president, would you vote for him?
- Should Yankee fans give George Steinbrenner the boot?
- Should Leona Helmsley go to jail?

Local radio helped to ensure maximum exposure for the program. Each Friday, the following week's question was faxed to participating radio stations along with key discussion sheets (points used by disk jockeys to hype the program). Each Tuesday afternoon, a "flash report" (midweek Yes/No cup count) was taken and reported to each participating radio station. Each Friday morning, Yes/No cup counts were taken in every store location. Results of the poll were also revealed to local media (radio stations), national media (USA Today), and announced via point-of-purchase in each 7-Eleven store the following Monday morning during the six weeks of the program.

Promotional support included:
- Radio: 7-Eleven purchased six-week radio schedules in designated markets. Schedules were weighted more heavily in the early part of the week to ensure that customers were aware of the question of the week. In addition, stations were asked to become Sound Off sponsors, which enabled 7-Eleven to get additional free time for teasers, personality involvement, and other promotional commitments such as listener call-ins, remotes, parties, and prizes.
- Newspaper shells were made available.
- Point of Sale: Each week, in-store signage displayed the new question of the week and the

result of the prior week's poll.

- Public Relations: On the Monday or Tuesday of each week prior to the start of a new question, there was a press briefing, with local celebrities and a followup with media to discuss the possible story angles.

Additional "jump-start" activities included a Sound Off Decision Kit, free beverage service in Yes/No cups for local government and civic meetings, a Sound Off decision coin, humorous story releases on Sound Off decisions, and "I Voted" cards for consumers.

RESULTS

The Sound Off program accomplished the following:

- Fountain Soft Drinks:
—+12 percent in units versus prior year.
—+16 percent in sales versus prior year.
—+15.7 percent in gross profit dollars versus prior year.
- Coffee:
—+2.1 percent in units versus prior year.
—+5.2 percent in sales versus prior year.
—+3.5 percent in gross profit dollars versus prior year.
- Sound Off received 33 percent more radio air time than purchased for a value of $1.3 million. This exceeded the 25 percent goal.
- Sound Off received approximately $1 million in nonpurchased, nonpaid print and TV exposure (for example, *USA Today*, "Larry King Show," etc.).

The program was extremely inexpensive, since cups and POS materials were regularly budgeted items. Best yet, both sales and profits were increased without product discounting.

1991-92

CAMPAIGN/EVENT
The Little Engine That Could

COMPANY
ShopKo Stores, Inc.

BRAND
Mass merchandise shopping

AGENCY
McCracken Brooks Communications, Inc.

YEAR
1991-92

BACKGROUND/MARKETING SITUATION

ShopKo was a leading mass merchandising retailer, with 110 stores in 13 states. It was a key player in most of its "B type" markets, cities with less than 100,000 population, and competed against Wal-Mart, Target, and Kmart.

"Predatory category killers," like Toys 'R' Us and wholesale clubs, had taken away sales from mass merchandisers. As they expanded into new cities, there was more head-to-head competition among mass merchandisers than ever before. ShopKo's customers were women ages 25 to 49. They had more children than typical competitors' customers, and enjoyed the shopping process more than competitors' customers. ShopKo could not afford to lose their loyalty.

OBJECTIVES

The measurable objective was to generate a 5 percent increase in store traffic and in sales volume at all ShopKo stores. Other objectives were to differentiate ShopKo from Kmart, Wal-Mart, and Target, and to reinforce ShopKo's image as an exciting place to shop for the holidays.

PROGRAM/STRATEGY

ShopKo envisioned a program with a positive message that would tie ShopKo to the values and aspirations of its target audience. Thus, the well-known children's book, *The Little Engine That Could*, was brought to life at ShopKo stores for a three-week period.

An exclusive The Little Engine That Could Fun Kit, containing a book, audiocassette, activity pages, stickers, puzzle, and poster, was created and offered for $5.99 with $25 in ShopKo purchases.

An instant-win sweepstakes game, Boarding Pass, gave consumers a chance to win more than one-half million prizes, including family vacations to Orlando, Florida, electric train sets, and exclusive *The Little Engine That Could* holiday ornaments. Boarding Pass game cards were attached to more than 4 million ShopKo circulars. Cards were also distributed at check-out and customer service counters. Consumers took their cards to interactive voice chip displays, then activated the chips on the displays. These triggered Little Engine train sounds and a voice that declared winners and their prizes. This was the first time that this type of display was used successfully in a retail environment.

Continuity support for the program included in-store signage, in-store radio messages, TV and radio commercials, circulars, and catalogs. To stimulate even more in-store excitement, additional programs, including a children's coloring contest, free engineer caps for children, and buttons, were developed. In all, more than 40 elements were developed.

RESULTS

The following were the results of the program:

- Sales for the promotional period broke the records, well ahead of the 5 percent objective and far ahead of 1990 performance.
- More than 50,000 Fun Kits were purchased, signaling endorsement of the promotion by customers.
- Interviews with store managers revealed that the promotion generated unprecedented consumer excitement and trade involvement.
- More than 10 million game cards were distributed.

1991-92

CAMPAIGN/EVENT
Free Ride

COMPANY
Western Union Financial Services Inc.

BRANDS
Western Union money transfers

AGENCY
Ryan Partnership

YEAR
1991-92

BACKGROUND/MARKETING SITUATION

Western Union had long been the leader in money transfer, the business of sending money by wire in a matter of minutes. The Western Union money transfer organization was actually a network of thousands of independently owned agencies. These agents demanded sound business reasons and immediate results to support promotional programs. Western Union faced two challenges. American Express was poised to enter the money transfer market in Chicago, and users of money transfer services usually resorted to wiring money only in emergencies. This forced purchasers to make spur of the moment decisions on how to send their money. Top-of-mind awareness and added value were critical to their decisions.

OBJECTIVES

Western Union needed a preemptive program that would reduce the impact of American Express in the key Chicago market. The objectives of the program were to:

- Build brand loyalty for Western Union and its independent agents.
- Heighten awareness in the targeted consumer segment more efficiently.
- Determine how the agent base could be leveraged to

optimize the efficiency and effectiveness for this particular program and for systemwide programs.

PROGRAM/STRATEGY

The program strategy consisted of the following elements:
- Broadcast media to reinforce the premise that Western Union was the most reliable way to send money by wire.
- Targeted media (spot TV, rail signage, radio) to create the doubt that other money transfer services were as reliable as Western Union.
- Target inner-city adults ages 29 to 49 who used mass transportation regularly in key consumer gathering locations.

Corresponding tactics were used to implement the strategy. Consumers who sent money through the Western Union network received a free roll of Chicago Transit Authority tokens, a $10 value, at point of sale. Many agents already sold these tokens, so the premium was an ideal offer. A fluctuating rebate was added to enable individual agents to match competitors' prices to various destinations.

Merchandising and media support consisted of:
- Spot television and radio in both English and Spanish.
- Multiple insertions in the *Chicago Sun-Times,* which had a higher readership among the target audience than other large-circulation Chicago newspapers.
- Extensive outdoor, mass transit, and in-store advertising. Point of sale included counter cards, posters, and tear-off pads.

To reward agents and counter personnel for recommending Western Union, an incentive program was also developed.

RESULTS

The results of the program were the following:
- Redemption rates for the Free Ride program were the highest ever for a money transfer program and were about 3 times the industry norm.
- The program dramatically reduced the impact of the American Express competitive entry. Some agents defected back to Western Union because they "were losing regular customers."
- Awareness and media coverage in Chicago were unprecedented. The *Chicago Sun-Times* reported significantly increased demand for newspapers carrying the program information.
- Advertising on city buses, on subways, and in train stations expanded awareness even further.
- Major media developed several news stories about the money transfer business and thus lent "top-spin" publicity.

The Free Ride program marked an important expansion of the promotion marketing discipline into a new arena beyond consumer packaged goods or financial services for affluent segments. Mass transit tokens were a sensible and tangible award that suited the wants, needs, and lifestyles of the targeted audience.

1991-92

CAMPAIGN/EVENT

Harvest of Good Foods

COMPANY

Campbell Soup Company/CSC Advertising

BRANDS

Multiple brands

YEAR

1991-92

BACKGROUND/MARKETING SITUATION

The Harvest of Good Foods had been a multibrand company promotion since 1984. However, as the company expanded its product lines and acquisitions, the effectiveness of the promotion had eroded. Many brands felt that the format of two FSI drops were either too cluttered (as many as 13 brands in an FSI) or thematically inappropriate for their audiences ("Back to School" in August and "Harvest" in October). On the other hand, the Campbell sales force did not want to surrender the trade impact of the program.

The challenge was compounded by the need to boost sales and volume on a stationary budget.

OBJECTIVES

The overall objective was to produce a program that would keep the impact of the original program intact while meeting the sales and volume goals of the individual brands. Campbell soup identified these specific objectives:

- Deliver a timely promotional umbrella theme creatively linking all participating brands and their products.
- Provide a flexible program format that encouraged creative themes and product combinations.
- Supply an informative and aggressive trade and sales force sell-in package.

- Increase overall trade participation in the promotion program by 20 percent.
- Obtain 100 percent of August, September, and October sales quotas on a national basis.

PROGRAM/STRATEGY

The following were key components of the program:

- Timing was held constant to allow comparison with prior years.
- The program was designed to allow all brands to participate, no matter how limited their budget or regionality.
- Four FSI drops were scheduled so all brands could promote when their products best fit their target consumer buying period. ROP alternatives were provided to either fill FSI gaps or maximize opportunities to tie-in trade specific events.
- The sales force was supplied with four top-of-mind trade and consumer themes, ensuring the best opportunity for trade support and consumer takeaway.
- Each FSI format contained a corporate page plus a full- and half-page ad for showcasing brands.
- A complete sales incentive package was distributed in May to assure maximum sell-in results for the August–November window. The package included funds for each region to conduct a market-by-market sales and trade merchandising contest.
- The program was translated at minimal cost to the military sales market.

RESULTS

The following were the results of the program:

- Volume attainment reached an all-time high, over 1 million cases of incremental sales. Even though the prior year had already been a record sales year, sales quota attainments were:
—August: 108 percent.
—September: 105 percent.
—October: 101 percent.
- The flexibility of the program gained participation by all key brands.
- Almost all regions reported trade participation increases in the range of 25 percent or more versus the prior year, with trade display and feature advertising the most prevalent forms of support.

1991-92

CAMPAIGN/EVENT
1991 Easter Open House/Photos with the Crayola Bunny

COMPANY
Hallmark Cards, Inc.

BRANDS
Hallmark Card Shops

AGENCY
SJI, Inc.

YEAR
1991-92

BACKGROUND/MARKETING SITUATION

Hallmark Cards was the longtime leader in the social expression industry. In 1991, the company focused its promotional efforts on supporting Hallmark Card Shops, the vast majority of which were independently owned and operated. Sales in the shops were seasonally influenced. Christmas, Valentine's Day, Mother's Day, and Easter received the majority of Hallmark promotional and advertising support.

The Hallmark Card Shops had a very loyal clientele. However, they faced increasing competition from other Hallmark distribution channels, such as supermarkets and drug stores, that were more convenient for some customers.

Hallmark needed to reinforce a point of difference between its cards shops and the other channels of distribution. The goal of any Hallmark promotion was to give customers an incentive to make a special trip to a Hallmark Card Shop. Because Easter fluctuates and tends to "sneak up" on people when it falls early in the year, as it did in 1991, it became a singular challenge to capture consumer attention early and drive traffic into the card shops.

OBJECTIVES

The Easter season is short when it falls early in the year. Since Easter fell on March 31 in 1991, Hallmark realized that consumers might be less inclined to plan ahead on purchases for the holiday. To defend against that possibility, objectives for the program were to:

- Increase traffic in Hallmark Card Shops during the short selling season.
- Generate repeat visits from consumers.
- Increase sales in Hallmark Card Shops.
- Increase awareness of the Crayola Bunny property, a property owned by Hallmark and available exclusively through

Hallmark Card Shops. Although the character was created by Hallmark in 1989 and the majority of Hallmark Easter specialty products related to the character, the "story" of the character had never been told to the public at large.

PROGRAM/STRATEGY

Hallmark made the Crayola Bunny character the point of difference between the Card Shops and other Hallmark channels. Utilizing this popular icon, Hallmark created the Easter Open House, a one-day event that took place in approximately 5,000 shops. The appeal of the Open House was the opportunity for customers to have their child's picture taken with the Crayola Bunny for free. The program consisted of the following elements:

- Free Photo Offer and Crayola Bunny Storybook: Free pictures with the Crayola Bunny were taken in designated photo areas set up in the card shops. A full-size Bunny costume provided by Hallmark was worn by a store employee. Photos were taken with 35mm film so customers had to return to the store to pick up the picture. Each photo was inserted in the cover of *Bunny Tales: The Adventure of Crayola Bunny and Friends* and given to the customer free of charge. Customers were required to revisit the store within five days to get their photos.
- Premium figurine: A premium figurine of Crayola Bunny and his friend Candy Cotton Tail, priced at $3.95 with a $5 purchase, was available from March 16 through March 30 at 4,000 Hallmark Gold Crown Card Shops. The figurine introduced the Candy Cotton Tail property, whose character was further developed in *Bunny Tales*. The premium offer was developed to increase the average size of purchase.
- Retail Sales Support Kit: Several other promotional elements, designed to support the national promotion effort by creating a festive atmosphere, were developed for Hallmark Card Shop owners. A kit explained how to hold a bunny coloring contest, a jelly bean counting contest, and two different "register to win" programs, one for a giant plush Crayola Bunny and one for a visit from Crayola Bunny.
- Advertising Support: During the week prior to Open House, advertisements included a :15 tag telling consumers about the Open House and the offer. Advertising in *Parade* magazine listed retailers making the offer.

RESULTS

A national sample of Hallmark Card Shops was surveyed to estimate results:

- Retailer support was high...88 percent of retailers believed that the Open House increased sales and in-store traffic above 1990 levels. Ninety percent wished to repeat the photo promotion in 1992.
- Customers responded well...72 percent of customers returned to pick up the free photo and storybook.
- Approximately 30 percent of consumers who returned made a purchase. For these customers, the average transaction was 13 percent higher than the average transaction during this period not related to the offer.
- In-store transactions during the Open House were 9 percent higher than during the 1990 Easter Open House.
- During the 1991 Open House weekend, sales were 13 percent higher than during the 1990 Open House weekend.
- During the final week before Easter, specialty transactions increased 15 percent over the same period in 1990.
- On Easter Sunday, dollar specialty sales increased 116 percent, and the number of specialty transactions increased 36 percent over Easter Sunday 1990.
- For the Easter selling season, dollar specialty sales increased 49 percent, and specialty transactions increased 18 percent over the 1990 Easter season.

1991-92

CAMPAIGN/EVENT
Drive Cleaner — Win A Beamer

COMPANIES
SuperAmerica Group, Inc., and Ashland Oil Company

BRAND
Super America 90 Octane Premium Unleaded

AGENCY
Promotion Works, Inc.

YEAR
1991-92

BACKGROUND/MARKETING SITUATION

SuperAmerica Group, a subsidiary of Ashland Oil, was a midwestern chain of gasoline and convenience stores. It operated approximately 360 stores, 135 of them in the Minneapolis–St. Paul area. In 1991, SuperAmerica offered consumers a choice of two unleaded gasoline products: 87 Octane Regular Unleaded or 92 Octane Premium Unleaded. The price per gallon differential was 12 cents.

Research had indicated the need for a gasoline that provided more power than regular unleaded but at a price below that of premium unleaded. In 1989, some oil companies responded to that need by introducing a midgrade 90 Octane unleaded gasoline. SuperAmerica entered this midgrade market in 1991 through a capital-intensive process that produced a midgrade product with clear advantages over the competition. In particular, the SuperAmerica 90 Octane Premium Unleaded featured a clean-air formulation that also met the BMW standards for intake valve cleanliness, the highest in the automotive industry.

OBJECTIVES

The objectives of the program were the following:
- Generate trial of 90 Octane.
- Increase share of product mix of 90 Octane.
- Expand SuperAmerica's share of total gasoline sales.

PROGRAM/STRATEGY

The following were the strategies of the program:

- Use an economic incentive to trade-up consumers of Regular Unleaded to 90 Octane.
- Leverage compliance with BMW intake valve cleanliness standards to gain product differentiation and superiority.
- Enlist store manager support to ensure fail-safe execution at the store level.
- Employ a combination of communication vehicles to generate consumer awareness of the promotion.

These strategies were implemented through use of the following tactics:

- A five-cent-per-gallon coupon was delivered via newspaper and in-store programs. The value of the coupon represented the cost difference between the two grades of gasoline.
- A random-draw sweepstakes offered consumers the chance to win a 1991 BMW 318i.
- A store manager incentive program awarded prizes for the largest gallon percentage increase over the base period.
- A media campaign including a four-color, double-truck newspaper ad and single-page newspaper ads, a :60 radio campaign, and point-of-sale materials.

RESULTS

The following were the results of the program:

- 90 Octane gallonage increased 227 percent.
- 90 Octane share of product mix more than doubled.
- SuperAmerica's total gasoline share also increased significantly.

This was a powerful promotion that clearly spelled "savings" without sacrificing quality in the minds of consumers.

1991-92

CAMPAIGN/EVENT

Tenth Anniversary Sweepstakes

COMPANY

The NutraSweet Company

BRAND

NutraSweet

AGENCY

The Hadley Group

YEAR

1991-92

BACKGROUND/MARKETING SITUATION

NutraSweet was an aspartame sweetener used in approximately 4,000 food products worldwide. In 1991, it was the largest branded name in grocery stores. The creative strategy for NutraSweet had been to convince consumers in a contemporary manner to like and prefer NutraSweet because it had a track record proven through use in thousands of products during the 10 years of its existence.

The NutraSweet Company's marketing challenge was unique. Its task was to create consumer demand for a product found only in other products. In addition, the company sales team was structured to focus its efforts on packaged foods manufacturers. Thus, the brand was marketed without the advantage of direct sales to the grocery trade.

OBJECTIVES

Because NutraSweet was not sold under its own branded name, this promotion placed heavy emphasis on developing brand name awareness, a function traditionally assigned to advertising. The objectives were to:

- Support new advertising and communicate the brand's ubiquity.
- Continue to build brand awareness.
- Support marketing partnerships with other products.

PROGRAM/STRATEGY

The strategy was to use the tenth anniversary of NutraSweet to create consumer awareness, interest, and

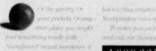

excitement. A national instant-win sweepstakes was developed for the anniversary celebration.

An FSI to 24 million consumers in top markets launched the program by announcing, "Looking for a free trip to Paris? Try the fridge." Consumers were asked to call an 800 phone number and punch in the UPC code from any NutraSweet sweetened product. This tactic permitted the involvement of more than two thousand brands, each with its own sales force. The phone-in sweepstakes identified valid UPC codes and randomly selected winners for the promotion's 18,001 prizes, ranging from a trip to any one of 50 countries where NutraSweet could be purchased, to gumball machines. The promotion used a unique, two-part, automated and live-operator telemarketing system to provide "winning" messages, "Sorry, try again" messages, and sales messages customized to the UPC code of the product used. Phone messages were recorded by the same talent that narrated the brand's general advertising television spots.

The use of UPC codes enabled the company to develop a national promotion without necessitating a sales force to promote the program through in-store merchandising.

RESULTS

While initially projecting 580,000 participants (assuming a 2 percent redemption rate on FSIs), the program generated over 1.5 million calls—more than three times the program's goals. In addition, the other objectives of the program were achieved, namely:

- It reinforced the advertising message.
- It promoted the brand's visibility.
- It strengthened ties with NutraSweet sweetened products through the simultaneous involvement of more than two thousand branded products with 18,000 SKUs.

Apparently, the NutraSweet Tenth Anniversary Sweepstakes was universally considered to be a promotion in good taste.

1991-92

CAMPAIGN/EVENT
Maalox Moments Radio Campaign

COMPANY
Rhone-Poulenc Rorer, a division of The Rorer Group

BRAND
Maalox

AGENCY
Local Marketing Corporation

YEAR
1991-92

BACKGROUND/MARKETING SITUATION

Maalox was a top-tier brand in the antacids category, competing for both the liquid and tablet segments. The goal was to make Maalox the "gold standard" for the category. However, retailer and competitive pressures had forced price discounting and sales allowances in order to increase display activity. Some of these practices had injured the brand's premium image and positioning at the retail level.

OBJECTIVES

Supporting the Maalox Moments national image advertising was the primary purpose of this campaign. Related to this were the needs for:

- An impactful retailer :30/:30 co-op radio program.
- Increased in-store and feature display activity.
- Maximized impact of available marketing dollars.

PROGRAM/ STRATEGY

The central creative strategy was a plan to identify common stressful situations as Maalox Moments and to offer a "fast relief" solution to consumers in the over-35 age group. This kind of memorable theme—one that would project the brand as the most

reliable product on the market—boosted by strong local market promotions would enhance the brand's image and lead to profits.

More than 180 consumer and trade promotions featuring Maalox moments were carried by demographically targeted, top radio stations in 35 local markets for a 15-week period. These encompassed local event sponsorship and sampling programs with stress- or food-related themes and account-specific promotions to increase store traffic and Maalox sales, thus adding value to the radio program.

Promotional themes included:

- Tax Time: Listeners could register to get "tax relief" and a chance to win cash from Maalox toward their tax bills. Elements included:
—Sampling and local radio personality appearances at post offices as consumers mailed their tax returns.
—Tax information centers at local retailers.
—Tax relief kits, including a tax guide and cassette, a Maalox sample, and a T-shirt.
—Maalox-sponsored tax seminars.
- Mother's Day: Concurrent with a May FSI drop, listeners were encouraged to send a letter describing the worst Maalox Moment they had given their mom or had had as a mom. Elements included:
—In-store registration for prizes.
—Gift certificates from Maalox retailers for perfume and flowers.
—Spa and getaway trips as grand prizes.
- Sports: Consumers identified those plays in the world of sports that had given them a Maalox Moment. Elements included:
—Moments identified during game broadcasts.
—Post-game analysis identifying Moments.
—Sports trivia Moments in sports contests.
—Pre- and post-game parties for special events.
- Summer Vacations: Summer vacation plans can be the source of some of the worst Maalox Moments. The company developed a summer vacation planning guide with advice and offers to help make vacations as stress-free as possible:
—Tips from the American Red Cross and AAA.
—Maalox coupons.
—Contest to win a family vacation for four.
—Retailer coupons for film processing.

RESULTS

The results of the program were:
- Eighty-six percent of Maalox retailers participated in the :30/:30 program.
- There was a 200 percent increase in account participation in the program.
- Around 300,000 Maalox samples were distributed.
- Over 1,000 stores displayed the vacation tips and 550,000 vacation guides were distributed overall.
- Maalox obtained over $1.1 million in free promotional spots, a value equivalent to 47 percent of the paid media buy.

1991-92

CAMPAIGN/EVENT
Team Spirit Program

COMPANY
Leaf, Inc.

BRANDS
Milk Duds, Heath Bar, Pay Day, Rainblo, Jolly Rancher

AGENCY
Berryman Communications Company

YEAR
1991-92

BACKGROUND/MARKETING SITUATION

Leaf marketed 18 candy brands and 9 gum brands. The corporation was America's sixth largest candy marketer with a 3.5 percent share of total candy dollars spent in the United States and a 5.1 percent dollar share of the chewing gum market. Its overall market share reflected a marketing strategy that avoided head-to-head competition with the giants of the industry and instead offered unique flavors or forms of products. A number of its brands were leaders within their segments, and all were parity priced with respect to the competition.

The category was growing, and there was increased pressure from the larger companies in the industry because they had budgets to sustain ongoing advertising that a company the size of Leaf could not match. But Leaf was not content with tombstone mentions and on-shelf price features.

OBJECTIVE

Leaf established a two-year objective to create a proprietary consumer promotion vehicle that would reach heavy users (children 6 to 18 years old) and purchasers (Moms) and:
- Support multiple brands.
- Build brand equity.
- Increase trial among nonusers.
- Offer incentives for continuity purchase.

PROGRAM/STRATEGY

The strategy was to develop a program that would provide financial and promotional support for Organized Youth Baseball Leagues, thereby strengthening Leaf's image and presence in this important part of its market.

The program enabled youth baseball leagues to earn money to purchase team equipment by saving and redeeming Leaf product wrappers. Each wrapper saved in the program was worth 15 cents towards the purchase of equipment. Leaf donated cents-off coupons to get teams started. A sweepstakes to win the opportunity to be celebrity bat boy or bat girl at a Major League Baseball game was an added incentive. This promotion was also modified to appeal to four levels of administration: headquarters executive staff, regional and state officers, local league presidents, and local team managers.

Specific plans for 1991 were to:
- Establish relationships with four of the top six Organized Youth Baseball Leagues.
- Create awareness and participation in the wrapper collection program—1,500 leagues for the 1991 season.
- Generate incremental sales through a continuity program.
- Build brand image.
- Generate nonpaid media publicity exposure through local media publicity.
- Secure relationships with sporting goods dealers.
- Create two databases to support the program for the long term.

A direct mail program to each league executive included a personalized letter, a five-minute video describing the program, a sample of Leaf products, and response cards that enabled executives to sign up local leagues. The response cards also asked the name of the local sporting goods dealer where equipment was purchased.

Participation by local leagues was further secured with recruitment help by league executives, signups at regional and state meetings, personalized direct mail, and updates on the wrapper program included in the league newsletters.

The program was announced in multiple media: Team Spirit mailings, *Sports Illustrated for Kids* magazine, and programs at Major League Baseball games. Nonpaid media included league newsletters and local media of participating leagues.

Following the league meetings and print announcements, a direct mail campaign to team sporting goods dealers was launched in two phases:
- Direct mail to team dealers, including a letter from the commissioner of Major League Baseball, a letter from Leaf's chairman of the board, a brochure, and a response card.
- Followup mailing that included a personalized kit of response cards and coupon sheets.

The National Sporting Goods Association, the largest sporting goods trade association in the nation, helped recruit team dealers. NSGA supported wrapper collection because it would increase member sales of baseball products. Leaf also gave NSGA the names of team dealers who were participating in the program but who were not NSGA members.

Because complicated redemption procedures can scuttle even the best continuity program, two key elements made wrapper collection very simple:
- Leaf provided league presidents with pre-addressed, postage-paid containers for shipping candy wrappers. Leaf handled fulfillment of all wrapper counting.
- The direct purchase of equipment avoided catalogs and order forms. Leaf simply made checks jointly payable to the league president and to a sporting goods dealer named by the team as their equipment supplier.

To track the program, Leaf created two databases: one for grassroots organized youth baseball executives, and one for team dealers who participated in the program.

RESULTS

The program was so well received that it far exceeded projections:

- Relationships were established with four of the six Organized Youth Baseball Leagues for both 1991 and 1992. In addition, endorsements came from regional Organized Youth Baseball officials who had never endorsed anything in the past.

- Both databases—of Youth Baseball executives and of team dealers—were established and became an integral part of Leaf concession programs.

- Response to the Leaf 1991 mailer to team dealers exceeded those generated by a 1990 FSI with 30 million circulation that had made roughly the same offer. The 1991 sweepstakes generated more than 35,000 responses.

- The Leaf bat boy/bat girl ad in *Sports Illustrated for Kids* generated a 4 percent response rate.

- In 1991, Leaf secured 258 sporting goods team dealers for the program. By early 1992, they were already heading for another winning season with 348 team dealers.

1991-92

CAMPAIGN/EVENTCAMPAIGN/EVENT
General Hospital Reintroduction
COMPANY
American Broadcasting Company
BRAND
The New General Hospital
AGENCY
Local Marketing Corporation
YEAR
1991-92

BACKGROUND/MARKETING SITUATION

ABC-TV's "General Hospital" was a daytime soap opera broadcast weekdays. In its time slot, it was one of two leading network programs among females ages 18 to 34, but viewership had declined significantly in recent years due to increased viewing alternatives. Competing non-network television programs, such as talk shows, game shows, and sitcom reruns, had cut into the program's viewership. Viewership had also declined because of the increase in the number of working women.

ABC revitalized the show by hiring a new producer and making several story and cast changes. The remade "General Hospital" needed to be introduced to a new generation of younger viewers. In addition, former viewers who had switched to non-network programming needed to be won back.

OBJECTIVES

The objectives of the program were the following:
• Increase trial, awareness, and viewership of the new program among women ages 18 to 34, with special emphasis on high school and college students just beginning their summer vacations.

- Increase the impact of the key market media buy.
- Position "General Hospital" as the "hot" soap opera to watch, especially during the reintroduction week of June 24.

PROGRAM/STRATEGY

Various combinations of six categories of events were executed in 14 local markets during a four-week period. These 14 different local executions, each consistent with national objectives, were implemented based on local media, retailer, and lifestyle considerations. These were important elements of the promotions:

- Radio was selected as the marketing medium.
- Radio personalities were made an integral part of promotions.
- To drive viewership, promotions were developed that required listeners to answer questions, give updates, or make predictions about the plot.
- Special events and local retailer tie-ins were developed. More than 50 promotions were executed for "General Hospital." These were grouped into six categories. The following examples from each category give some sense of the scope of this program.
- General Hospital Set Promotions included Touch 'n' Go to the "General Hospital" Set (Station WCKZ, Charlotte): Listeners were urged to tune into "General Hospital" to see which character had the first kiss of the day. The first caller for each day was registered to go to the local mall and continuously touch a life-size cutout of "General Hospital" heart throb Mac Scorpio for the Touch 'n' Go finals. The contestant who touched the cutout the longest won a trip to the "General Hospital" set in Los Angeles. The station phoned in live, on-air "progress reports" every hour, until only one contestant was left, having touched Mac for 28 hours!
- Retail Tie-Ins included The New "General Hospital" White Sales (Station WBZZ, Pittsburgh): The station asked listeners questions about each week's episodes and invited them to register their answers at all eight departments in Hornes Department Stores to win a trip to the "General Hospital" set. Posters were displayed in-store, and the event was announced in Hornes local newspaper ads. A radio station personality appeared at Hornes stores, awarding prizes to customers who could correctly answer questions about General Hospital episodes.
- Viewing Parties included Join the fun at the "General Hospital" Viewing Party at Quincy's (Station KHMX, Houston): The station hosted a viewing part at Quincy's AM, a local nightclub. The party featured "General Hospital" broadcast on TV monitors, wheelchair races, and "Most Creative CPR" contests. The club was decorated in a hospital motif, and "General Hospital" trivia question winners were awarded prizes throughout the evening.
- "General Hospital" Updates included Instant Recaps of the New "General Hospital" (Station WPGC, Washington, D.C.): The station invited listeners to tune in to "General Hospital" for a chance to give an on-air review. Callers were asked to give a :60 creative review of the previous day's show to win "General Hospital" merchandise and to qualify for a grand prize.
- Story Line and Character Trivia Quizzes included The "General Hospital" Makeover (Station WKRQ, Cincinnati): The first listener to fax in the correct answer to a daily quiz on characters and romances received "General Hospital" prizes. A grand prize daily winner was drawn to receive an "afternoon affair" at a prestigious beauty salon, as well as a Saturday night stay for two at a downtown hotel, among other prizes.
- Miscellaneous events included How Is Your Life Like a Soap Opera? (Station WYTZ, Chicago): Listeners called in to describe their own true life soap operas. The Grand Prize was a trip to Los Angeles to visit the "General Hospital" set.

RESULTS

The following were the results of the program:

- A 25 percent share increase in measured markets versus a 4 percent increase in nonradio markets.
- A 14 percent ratings increase for General Hospital in measured markets.
- More than 3,000 free promotional spots valued at $296,000 ran over and above the base media buy.
- ABC received an additional $55,000 in promotional radio airtime and 580 announcements more than were originally committed by the station.

This was the first promotion of its kind ever done for a daytime soap opera, although radio advertising was common for TV. The ABC "General Hospital" promotion reached its target audience for two significant reasons. First, it permitted access to local market radio personalities who play important roles in influencing the opinions of young consumers. Second, it did not passively ask viewers to tune in to "General Hospital" but challenged them to participate in the program in various creative ways.

1992-1993

REGGIE

AWARDS

CAMPAIGN

SOVIET UNION GOING OUT OF BUSINESS SALE — BARQ'S, INC.

D-DAY — FRITO-LAY INC.

CRAYOLA COLORING BOOK TIE-IN — BINNEY & SMITH INC.

IT'S UP TO YOU! — EMERY WORLDWIDE

FOOTLOCKER '92 — THE QUAKER OATS COMPANY

KEYSTONE BEER FISHING HOTLINE — COORS BREWING COMPANY

THE TALE OF THE TAPE INSTANT-WIN GAME — MEMTEK PRODUCTS

YOU'RE THE STAR AT NATWEST — NATIONAL WESTMINSTER BANK

COMIC RELIEF V AND COMEDY CENTRAL BOOT CAMP — WARNER-LAMBERT COMPANY

TALKIN' CAN SWEEPSTAKES — COORS BREWING COMPANY

1992-93

CAMPAIGN/EVENT
Soviet Union Going Out of Business Sale

COMPANY
Barq's, Inc.

BRAND
Barq's Root Beer

YEAR
1992-93/Super Reggie

BACKGROUND/MARKETING SITUATION

With a 0.5 percent market share and a national advertising budget of less than $3 million, Barq's Root Beer, the nation's number-two root beer brand, was yet a tiny player in the carbonated soft drink business. Barq's distribution in the United States was approaching 70 percent, new opportunities for growth by geographic expansion were dwindling, and it was becoming evident that the next focus should be increasing per capita consumption in existing markets.

Barq's promotions had to work within certain parameters dictated by competing with better entrenched, better financed competitors. Any promotion had to benefit Barq's largest unit package sizes, provide high perceived value at low cost, generate substantial publicity to supplement paid media, and drive secondary retail display throughout the peak summer months.

OBJECTIVES

Objectives for the promotion were numerous and intimately linked. They included:

- Acceptance by at least 80 percent of the Barq's bottling network, 98 percent of which were bottlers of either Coca-Cola or Pepsi and accustomed to the

interest and efficiencies of the promotions generated by these two giants of the industry.

- Expanding interest from Barq's core consumers, ages 12 to 24, to supermarket shoppers ages 18–49, those most likely to purchase 12-packs and two-liter bottles.
- Generating publicity in national electronic and print media.
- Achieving 15,000 incremental retail displays of 12-packs and two-liter bottles.
- Increasing market share and sales growth 50 percent above industry trends.
- Two to three percent consumer redemption of the first on-pack offer ever.

PROGRAM/STRATEGY

The promotion strategy was to create an event too big to be ignored.

For more than 70 years, Soviet Communism had ruled much of Asia and Eastern Europe, launched a Cold War, and pushed nuclear proliferation. Then, on December 25, 1991, it disappeared. Seizing upon the phenomenal nature of this event, 10 days later Barq's announced its tongue-in-cheek Soviet Union Going Out of Business Sale, declaring that "Gorby's loss is your gain" and explaining how consumers could receive free pieces of Communist memorabilia for two proofs-of-purchase from specially marked two-liter bottles of Barq's Root Beer beginning May 1, 1992.

With claims of "they've lost their lease and everything must go" and "they're selling out to the bare walls," promotional packaging, point-of-purchase pieces, and TV and radio ads were introduced. The media announced the event through *Newsweek, The Wall Street Journal,* "ABC World News This Morning," AP and UPI International wires, NPR, and hundreds of local newspapers and radio and TV stations. With all this publicity, jaded bottlers and retailers eagerly snapped up the program for the summer.

All that remained was to acquire an inventory of "Soviet Stuff" and "Communist Party Favors" ranging from sloganeering znachki pins to working telephones snatched by black marketeers from Kremlin offices in the days following the coup attempt. A shopping trip to Moscow in late January landed roughly 800,000 pieces of Soviet memorabilia that were delivered to the United States by April. Consumers could receive collections of pins, postage stamps, and commemorative ribbons through the on-pack offer, while bottlers and retailers were motivated with collectibles like phones and army officers' hats. Barq's bottlers ultimately erected 30,000 displays despite concurrent promotions by Coke and Pepsi.

RESULTS

Every objective was exceeded by a wide margin:
- Of all root beers, only Barq's increased market share in the 1992 summer season.
- Fully 98 percent of Barq's bottlers supported the event.
- Sales growth achieved double-digit gains.
- The 15,000 displays projected grew into 30,000 actual displays.
- Estimated value for publicity topped $2.5 million.
- Consumer redemptions rose to 4.5 percent.
- The promotion ran nearly 20 weeks on the strength of material and packaging reorders.

As an example of creativity, topicality, and problem solving within tight constraints, the Soviet Union Going Out of Business Sale was uncommon in the extreme. As an event of socially significant proportions in its own right, it will assume its rightful position in history.

1992-93

CAMPAIGN/EVENT
D-Day

COMPANY
Frito-Lay Inc.

BRANDS
Doritos® Nacho Cheese, Cool Ranch, Taco, Jumpin' Jack Cheese

AGENCY
Tracy-Locke Promotional and Regional Marketing

YEAR
1992-93

BACKGROUND/MARKETING SITUATION

With more than $1 billion in annual retail sales and more than 75 percent share in the flavored tortilla chip category, Doritos had held a dominant position in the snacks industry since 1966. Popular Nacho Cheese flavor Doritos represented more than 60 percent of the brand's volume.

Regional brands and private labels were striving to wrest shelf space from Doritos with aggressive price-offs. Wishing to avoid a price war, Frito-Lay sought an added-value alternative for consumers. It was determined that the most compelling added value would be quality enhancement, so a relaunch for Nacho Cheese flavor that would announce a cheesier chip was planned. But what would be the best way to stage the relaunch?

OBJECTIVES

The following objectives were identified:
- Deliver a product enhancement message to consumers.
- Drive trial and awareness of the relaunched product.
- Gain display space at retail.

PROGRAM/STRATEGY

Frito-Lay opted for a sampling program with a novel twist: its own employees would organize into sampling teams for a one-day nationwide sampling event on Saturday, May 2, 1992, Doritos Day (D-Day for short). Fifty D-Day captains selected from Frito-Lay field personnel received information on how to organize and direct sampling teams, sampling budgets, coupons, and consumer giveaways for their teams.

More than 10,000 supermarkets and 100 regional events were targeted for sampling. Retailers hosted sampling in their parking lots. In-store displays were authorized based on the availability of on-premise sampling, couponing, and point-of-purchase materials. Radio remote broadcasts were employed in communities where 250 or more Frito-Lay employees resided. Frito-Lay manufacturing employees enjoyed special invitations to the events, as rewards for producing the new flavor.

Two days prior to D-Day, Frito-Lay ran a full-page ad in *USA Today*. It starred a number of employees involved in planning the events.

RESULTS

D-Day was a success on many levels:

- More than 6 million bags of Nacho Cheese flavor Doritos and coupons were distributed in one day. If a sampling service had been hired, it would have cost nearly $4 million.
- The number of stores that displayed Doritos rose 14 percent, and the number of stores with secondary displays increased 13 percent.
- More than $6 million in incremental dollar sales were earned.
- Five-dollar share points were gained, and four-pound share points were gained.
- Coupon redemption rates averaged a high of 35 to 40 percent.
- Key market radio/merchandising actualized a value of almost twice that of the buy.

Perhaps the greatest gains were intangible. More than 13,000 Frito-Lay employees joined in this sampling effort. Empowerment and pride in ownership gave Doritos its most motivated product spokespeople ever and, coincidentally, the largest sampling effort ever undertaken on one day.

1992-93

CAMPAIGN/EVENT

Crayola Coloring Book Tie-In

COMPANY

Binney & Smith Inc.

BRANDS

Crayola Changeable Markers

AGENCY

Fresh Perspective, Inc.

YEAR

1992-93

BACKGROUND/MARKETING SITUATION

Since its founding in 1903, Binney & Smith, the originators of Crayola Crayons, had expanded its product base to a wide array of children's creative tools: colored pencils, chalk, water paints, fabric paints, art and activity kits, and markers.

The Crayola brand name had 98 percent unaided awareness with children and moms and was the undisputed leader in every category in which the brand competed. Gradually, however, toys in other categories, especially video games and action figurines, were beginning to usurp time from the 25 minutes per day that children devoted to coloring.

Binney & Smith recognized the challenge, but Binney & Smith was not a large company. Traditionally, a major portion of its limited promotion dollars had to be assigned to FSIs during key sell-in periods. Another small company threatened by giants in the toy industry may have been daunted by the magnitude of the task of retrieving lost share, but Binney & Smith had 90 years of survival experience backing its one-person promotion department.

OBJECTIVES

Binney & Smith outlined its objectives as follows:
- Increase product usage.
- Generate trial of new products.
- Increase number and quality of feature ads and displays.
- Initiate holiday merchandising earlier in the season.
- Use promotion dollars more efficiently.
- Create annual turn-key promotions that require minimal execution by the internal promotion department.

PROGRAM/STRATEGY

To increase product usage, Binney & Smith enlisted tie-in partners in a 20-page solo FSI designed as a coloring book. Coupons ran across the bottom on perforated strips along with a brand sell message. The special-order uncoated stock was perfect for coloring. A holiday story incorporating specific reference to each participating brand replaced the usual promotional sell copy. That, plus the four-color printing, restricted to depicting the brand on each page only, gave each product riveting visibility. As the story flowed from page to page, the consumer was rewarded with a gratifying sense of added value. To generate trial, the coloring book carried a sweepstakes overlay with a free bounceback offer for new Crayola Changeable Markers.

Trade performance was encouraged with a national in-store coloring contest. Coloring book tear-off entry pads with four different scenes were printed with individual store logos. The Binney & Smith sales force worked with retailers to award prizes to contest winners. Binney & Smith reasoned that the trade would be motivated to support the event because a promotion including 20 products promised additional sales storewide. The participating big name brands would also leverage front-page placement on circulars and would help defray costs for in-store activities.

RESULTS

The Crayola coloring book went to 54 million households and was so well received that Valassis established the event for a drop each November to usher in the holidays. More than 500,000 new Changeable Markers and 40¢ coupons were distributed to children, and more than 275 key accounts supported the coloring contest. For the price of one FSI page, Crayola received exposure on 20 pages and then enjoyed even more exposure on 2 million tear-off pads. This promotion was a textbook example of a simple idea exploited to its fullest potential.

1992-93

CAMPAIGN/EVENT

It's Up To You!

COMPANY

Emery Worldwide

AGENCY

QLM Associates, Inc.

YEAR

1992-93

BACKGROUND/MARKETING SITUATION

In 1989, Emery, noted for its business-to-business heavyweight air freight services, was purchased by Consolidated Freightways, Inc., to form Emery Worldwide, a Consolidated Freightways Company. Prior to the purchase, Emery tried to shift its marketing focus from heavyweight air freight to the air express delivery category. The new company continued this marketing thrust, but lost market share in the attempt. Research revealed that its strength was based not only on its ability to carry heavyweight cargo, but also on its flexible scheduling: "customer-ization" was its niche. By 1992, some former Emery customers still were alienated by the strategic change. Even Emery's own employees were confused.

OBJECTIVES

The primary objective was to recover lapsed customers. Secondary objectives were to:

- Communicate Emery's full-service network and customized service.
- Communicate to customers and employees that Emery's focus had returned to deliveries of freight weighing five pounds and more.
- Give salespeople new tools and incentives to sell Emery services.

PROGRAM/STRATEGY

Emery launched the program to its account managers with a sales incentive packet that announced the theme, It's Up To You! This packet contained customer sales presentation information that detailed Emery's full-service national and international capabilities and its flexibility to deliver customized service. It also extended suggestions for regaining lapsed customers, but the best sales tool it supplied was a customer discount of 50 percent off the first retrial shipment, up to $250. To keep the program foremost in everyone's mind, It's Up To You! posters were displayed in all Emery terminals, and stickers were affixed to all retrial shipments, which singled them out for special attention during the freight handling process.

Following the packet, Emery asked account managers to each name his or her 25 most profitable lapsed customers they could target for retrial during a three-month period. During that time, to encourage customer sales, account managers could earn 1 percent of all revenues gained after the initial retrial period.

RESULTS

This simple program generated $3.8 million, the equivalent of adding one full day to Emery's operating year, while the cost to implement the program was merely 4 percent of the incoming revenue. It was the first time that Emery had ever offered a revenue-sharing incentive, and the company was so pleased that it planned three more promotions for 1993. Significantly, the program clarified Emery's mission to its customers and employees and taught a valuable lesson about teamwork in action.

1992-93

CAMPAIGN/EVENT
Footlocker '92

COMPANY
The Quaker Oats Company

BRAND
Gatorade

AGENCY
Marketing Corporation of America (MCA)

YEAR
1992-93

BACKGROUND/MARKETING SITUATION

With an 85 percent share of the market, Gatorade was easily the nation's leading sports beverage in 1992. The summer months, June through August, were the peak season for Gatorade. All efforts were concentrated on developing new promotions that would ensure display support and would top previous records for sales to target males, ages 18 to 24.

OBJECTIVES

Summer objectives for Gatorade were:

CONSUMER
To increase volume by driving up the transaction size and purchase frequency.

TRADE
To achieve aggressive levels of in-store display support, primarily in grocery and convenience stores.

PROGRAM/STRATEGY

To reach consumers, the brand elected to find a tie-in partner willing to fund an added value offer on the Gatorade package. A dealer loader program was chosen as the best avenue to motivate the trade.

The brand approached Footlocker athletic footwear stores, which did indeed agree to fund a $10 on-pack savings certificate redeemable on any purchase of $50 or more at Footlocker

and Lady Footlocker outlets. Footlocker also agreed to honor a $25 gift certificate offered to Gatorade buyers for every 50 cases of Gatorade displayed (maximum of 300 cases or six certificates).

Because Gatorade and Footlocker shared the same target audiences and the same peak seasons, they both eagerly pooled all resources to launch this $1 billion event across all channels:

- A $10 savings certificate offer on 100 million bottles of Gatorade.
- Tags on national TV commercials during prime-time hours including the Olympics.
- Full-page ads in *Sports Illustrated* and *People* magazines.
- Full-page FSI to 47 million households highlighting the $10 offer and dropping a 55¢ coupon.
- Top radio stations in over 20 markets ran spots and were provided with $80,000 in Footlocker certificates to give away to secure incremental radio merchandising.
- Over 2 million Gatorade 25¢ coupons were distributed through Footlocker outlets and by Gatorade van sampling.
- Static clings and 3-D header cards drove impulse sales in grocery and C-stores, supported further by ActMedia cart signage throughout July.
- A "shoe box" mailing of program details and a Gatorade squeeze bottle went to trade publications in custom-made Gatorade/Footlocker shoe boxes.

RESULTS

Consumer response was the largest ever for Gatorade and Footlocker. More than 1 million consumers used Gatorade label certificates to purchase more than $50 million in Footlocker merchandise. Three quarters of the way into the program, Footlocker redeemed $5.2 million on the Gatorade coupon, resulting in $41 million worth of retail sales. Gatorade also achieved new distribution in Woolworth stores (Footlocker's parent company) with a $500,000 order. Equally important, display levels for Gatorade were the highest in the juice category at 50 percent. Combining the resources of two companies with complementary products made this one of the hottest promotions of the summer of 1992.

1992-93

CAMPAIGN/EVENT
Keystone Beer Fishing Hotline

COMPANY
Coors Brewing Company

BRANDS
Keystone, Keystone Light, and Keystone Dry beers

AGENCY
McCracken-Brooks Communications, Inc.

YEAR
1992-93

BACKGROUND/MARKETING SITUATION

In 1989, Coors Brewing Company introduced Keystone and Keystone Light beers, followed by Keystone Dry in 1990. By 1992, the three brands accounted for more than 10 percent of the volume in the popular-priced beer category and were sold in all 50 states through liquor, grocery, and convenience stores.

The popular-priced category was itself growing and accounted for 16 percent of the total beer category in 1992, up from 13 percent in 1991. The chief competitors to Keystone were Miller's Old Milwaukee and Budweiser's Busch.

Research conducted by Keystone had indicated that Keystone drinkers were typically males ages 25 to 54 who enjoyed the outdoors, specifically hunting and fishing. More than 80 percent of the 40 million licensed fishermen in the United States were males 25 to 54 years old, too.

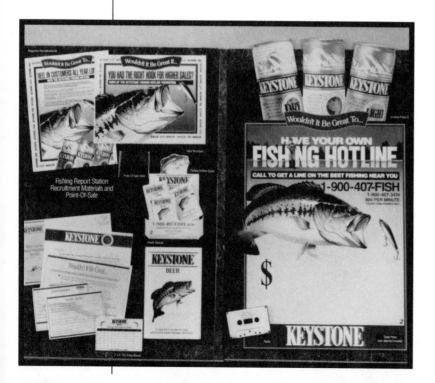

OBJECTIVES

Because the Keystone brand was so young and the category was so volatile, Coors needed to aggressively stimulate consumer, trade, and sales force involvement.

Consumer goals focused on developing brand equity:
- Generate trial and awareness.
- Enhance Keystone brand positioning: "Bottled Taste of Beer in a Can."
- Provide a point-of-difference that generated interest and purchase continuity among the target audience.
- Build long-term brand loyalty.
- Reinforce Coors' commitment to the outdoors and to environmental preservation.

With the trade, the goals were

stocking 12- and 24-packs of all three Keystone beers, plus display and feature ad support.

The sales force needed incentives, too:

- Push for more display and feature ad support.
- Increase distribution of point-of-purchase materials among the trade.
- Increase sales volume.
- Fill distribution, especially on Keystone Dry.

PROGRAM/STRATEGY

In the past, other beer brands had dabbled in fishing promotions, but never on an ongoing basis. Coors imagined a continuity program that would grow with the Keystone brand name and around which periodic consumer events could be staged. A perfect vehicle for this strategy was found in a national 900 number pay-per-call service.

Coors' Keystone Fishing Hotline was the first such service to offer current species-specific fishing information all year long. For only 60 cents per minute, anglers could learn where the fish were biting in over 500 locales across the country. More than 2,500 individual species reports were collected from bait and tackle shops and from outdoor guides each week. In exchange, these businesses, designated Official Keystone Reporting Stations, were identified at the end of each report. Callers had two options for retrieving fishing tips: (1) turn to the automatic menu or (2) dial a four-digit Quick Code assigned to individual states and regions. A typical three-minute call could cost $1.80—a fair price to the consumer because Coors chose not to operate the hotline as a profit center.

The Keystone Fishing Hotline operated out of St. Cloud, Minnesota. An outbound telemarketing center employing 25 people captured, updated, and recorded fishing reports each week. The 500 reporting stations had been recruited via print ads in industry publications and direct mail. They received procedural manuals and reporting forms. Consumers received Hotline Guides at sport shows and at point-of-purchase.

The hotline proved to be an ideal umbrella event around which three seasonal promotions were delivered:

- Spring $5 cash rebate: up to $5 cash rebate toward a fishing license with purchase of 12- or 24-packs.
- Summer $6 discount on membership in the North American Fishing Club (NAFC).
- Fall fishing calendar: a 1993 calendar for $5.95 with the purchase of any Keystone beer.

RESULTS

Although determining the long-term results of the program would have been premature, first-year results were notably encouraging:

- Point-of-sale placement for the hotline was between 20 percent and 30 percent higher than realized by any previous Keystone promotion. Money was reallocated to the point-of-purchase budget from advertising because trade support proved so strong.
- Seventy percent of callers used the hotline several times, and 20 percent called six or more times.
- Keystone became positioned as the official beer of licensed anglers. Further evidence that the target market was reached was compiled from data revealing that the majority of callers were males, average age 37 years, and that 79 percent of callers described the hotline information as useful.
- In sales volume measurements, 18 percent of callers said the hotline had increased their purchasing intent of Keystone beer, and 14 percent reported that they had been unaware of the brand prior to the hotline.

This promotion positioned Keystone as the "official beer" among the estimated 40 million licensed anglers and gave Keystone a respectable way to strike a responsive chord among men.

1992-93

CAMPAIGN/EVENT
The Tale of the Tape Instant-Win Game

COMPANY
Memtek Products

BRANDS
Memorex blank audio and video tapes

AGENCY
Harwood Marketing Group

YEAR
1992-93

BACKGROUND/MARKETING SITUATION

Memtek Products, a subsidiary of Tandy Corporation, marketed Memorex audio and video tapes. Although Memtek did not lead in the blank audio and video tape categories, it had very high "top of mind" awareness for superior quality.

In the cramped retail environment of the blank tape categories, shelf space was limited and display space was almost nonexistent. Video tapes had become a commodity business, while audio tapes maintained brand loyalty. The category's most critical sales period was the August/Back-to-School season when students "loaded" product. Because every manufacturer used trade allowances and prices were at parity during this season, Memtek needed a tiebreaker to clinch sales.

OBJECTIVES

Consumer objectives aimed at sales and loyalty:

- Increase sales seven percent over previous year sales.
- Present a point of difference that could outmaneuver the competition at point of purchase.
- Give added value to the package.
- Develop continuity.

Trade objectives emphasized display space:
- Generate merchandising support for pre-packed shipper displays.
- Create enthusiasm among buyers and store managers.

PROGRAM/STRATEGY

Providing added value was the only way to take the focus off the price in this atmosphere of heavy price discounting. The answer was a novel instant-win sweepstakes that Memtek devised, which had all hopes riding upon its success. Consumers learned via package bursts, insert cards, and display header cards that they might win a $5,000 concert trip of their choice by purchasing specially marked Memorex audio and video tapes. Then, before recording, they could listen or watch for radio and TV personality Rick Dees on each tape. He appeared on five seeded winning tapes only. For continuity, consumers who mailed in 10 proofs of purchase would receive a free audio tape. There was no advertising to support this promotion. It stood on its own merit.

The sell-in to the trade was preceded by more fanfare. Key buyers were mailed an oversized replica of a Memorex audio cassette with instructions to pull the "tape" out of the cassette. A message printed on the tape explained the promotion and made every buyer a winner. Prizes were the $5,000 concert trip, a Memorex rack stereo system, or a Memorex personal stereo.

RESULTS

More than 15,000 pre-pack displays were produced, and overall sales were 12 percent higher than sales of the previous year. October turned into a month of record sales, achieved without price discounting. Memtek attributed the success of this promotion to the use of a celebrity spokesperson, the teaser mailing that made each buyer a winner, and the attention-getting displays at retail.

1992-93

CAMPAIGN/EVENT

You're the Star at NatWest

COMPANY

National Westminster Bank

AGENCY

Communications Diversified

YEAR

1992-93

BACKGROUND/MARKETING SITUATION

In 1992, NatWest had 264 branches in New York and New Jersey. Although the bank was respected for its fiscal stability and personalized customer service, the banking industry as a whole was suffering from negative publicity and a weak economy. NatWest was in a strong position relative to its competitors. Nonetheless, many of its personal banking customers kept only one account there, while their lines of credit and installment loans were with rival institutions. NatWest business accounts established checking or credit with NatWest but sent deposit and investment banking elsewhere. These were two sources of lost income.

NatWest was aware that automatic teller machines and unfavorable press had undermined traditional face-to-face banking relationships that had once given customers the confidence to entrust all their business to a single bank. NatWest needed to motivate its customers to speak with bank personnel to pinpoint customer needs, establish strong personal relationships, and sell more services. Looking at the ascendancy of promotional marketing in the banking industry, NatWest saw a dual opportunity. It could distinguish itself from its competitors by adding some enjoyment to the banking routine, and it could expand its level of service to existing customers.

OBJECTIVES

This promotion had clear objectives tied into the bank's 1992 goals:

- Draw more existing customers into NatWest branches to talk face-to-face with a customer service representative.
- Motivate existing customers to do more business with NatWest.
- Help each branch achieve its annual revenue goals.

- Create an atmosphere of involvement, fun, and friendliness in each branch to encourage better customer relations.

PROGRAM/STRATEGY

Movies have broad appeal, and the window for this promotion ran from late March (the Academy Awards) through the release period for summer movies. NatWest chose to borrow on the equity of our national fascination with movies by staging a promotion titled You're the Star at NatWest.

First was Direct Mail and Direct Attention: An April month-long mailing to 880,000 small business customers and consumers invited them to visit any NatWest branch. The outer envelope proclaimed "You're halfway to Hollywood. Look for your winning tickets inside." Inside were a listing of NatWest branches, a brochure, and half a movie ticket. The recipient carried the half ticket to any branch to see if numbers on the piece matched those on a display. The display replicated an old-fashioned theater ticket window.

Each customer's half ticket awarded at least an usher's seat finder pen light. A bank employee greeted winners and directed each to a customer service representative to redeem the half ticket for the prize. Customers could then enter a second sweepstakes, called the Comeback Sweepstakes, by answering a few questions about their service needs on a Customer Relationship Outline. Noncustomers received the sweepstakes packet upon entering the bank.

Customer service representatives were trained to engage customers in conversation and to help them complete the outline. Thus each customer enjoyed personalized attention and learned NatWest's full range of services.

Other elements of the program included:
- Fun and Games: Each bank received a life-size cutout of Humphrey Bogart, a Polaroid camera, film, and picture frames. On Matinee Days, customers could receive a framed Polaroid picture of themselves with Bogie. To maximize the excitement of the promotion, branches were encouraged to stage movie-themed events and contests, such as:
—Movie trivia contests, star search talent contests, star look-alike contests, Academy Awards guess-the-winners contests.
—Humphrey Bogart Look Alike Day.
- Prize Structure: The Grand Prize for both sweepstakes was a trip for two to Hollywood, including a walk-on part in a major motion picture. The five first prize winners each received a 32-inch Sony TV; 10 Panasonic Palmcorder video cameras were second prizes. The Comeback Sweepstakes awarded a 19-inch Toshiba TV at each branch.
- Top Producer Gala: All 400 employees of the 27 highest-achieving branches were honored with their guests at a star-studded major movie preview staged at New York's Ziegfeld Theater and the adjacent New York Hilton.

Winning branches were determined by the number of new products and services sold as a percentage of customers who redeemed their sweepstakes half tickets. Branches that submitted the most Customer Relationship Outlines as a percentage were also eligible to attend.

RESULTS

Branch visitors who brought their half tickets totalled 12.5 percent of NatWest's customers. The number of new products and services exceeded goals.

Incremental funds and other specific data were confidential information that could not be released. However, the originality and careful execution of this event were impressive. In particular, the training program for bank personnel in all branches was comprehensive, effective, and unusual for any promotion in any industry, not simply in banking.

1992-93

CAMPAIGN/EVENT
Comic Relief V and Comedy Central Boot Camp

COMPANY
Warner-Lambert Company

BRAND
Certs

AGENCY
Wunderman Cato Johnson

YEAR
1992-93

BACKGROUND/MARKETING SITUATION

The breath mints category was highly concentrated and dominated by Breathsavers, Tic Tac, and Certs. Of these three leaders, Certs held a 21 percent share compared to Breathsavers and Tic Tac, which were neck-and-neck at 12 percent respectively. Certs was distributed in the food, drug, convenience store, and mass merchandise classes of trade.

In an attempt to contemporize the brand and to regain consumer share of mind, Certs had recently launched new advertising using comedians Rita Rudner, Bobby Collins, and Richard Jeni. But Certs also needed to grab the attention of retail trade partners and the Warner-Lambert sales force.

CERTS 3-Pack with Mini-Mints

In-Pack Survival Guide

OBJECTIVES

These were simple and in keeping with a brand maintaining its position as first in its category:
- Consumer: gain incremental and repeat purchase.
- Trade: gain incremental display and feature.
- Sales Force: increase sell-in, raise motivation.
- Leverage the comedy positioning for more exposure throughout all communications.

PROGRAM/STRATEGY

The brand introduced a comedy campaign in two phases.

PHASE I
Phase I, Comic Relief V, from May through September, involved Certs as sponsor for the fifth all-star

comedy event to raise funds and awareness about the plight of America's homeless. Hosted by Billy Crystal, Robin Williams, and Whoopi Goldberg, Comic Relief V featured the country's best comedians.

A teaser packet titled Something's Funny Going On Around Here was mailed to the Certs sales force two weeks before the national sales meeting, preparing them for the promotion. A sell-in video premiered at the meeting. It featured Comic Relief President, Bob Zmuda, and hilarious clips from the past Comic Relief shows.

For consumer excitement, the World's Funniest Sweepstakes awarded 100 grand prize trips for two on the exclusive Certs Comic Relief Cruise on Carnival Cruise Lines, plus over 100,000 other prizes. Dedicated floor stands were displayed at point of purchase, with counter units for convenience stores.

On the local level, comedy club events were co-sponsored by Certs and HBO in 44 markets. Radio stations were offered the CERTified Laugh Pack, a duffle bag designed like a roll of Certs and packed with a Comic Relief sweatshirt, T-shirt, and Certs samples. The comedy clubs and radio stations supported Comic Relief with a blitz of recognition and their own contests. Local comedy club events were linked to account-specific promotions. Comic Relief V was also broadcast live on HBO on May 16 under Certs' title sponsorship. The Certs logo was visible throughout the five-hour broadcast. Certs national TV spots urged viewers to support the cause. Certs' radio buy promoted the sweepstakes, the local club events, and retail account tie-ins.

PHASE II

Phase II, from October through December, included a tie-in with TV's Comedy Central and Comedy Boot Camp, where consumer winners would be drilled in the basics of stand-up comedy by top comedians. The event was subsequently given a TV debut on Comedy Central's Short Attention Span Theater.

This was also launched with a teaser mailing to the sales force. This time the packet featured a cartoon drill sergeant demanding, "I want you to make me laugh." Enclosed was a set of dog tags embossed with the sales rep's name and "In Training for Comedy Central Boot Camp."

The drill sergeant was subsequently transferred to retail point of purchase materials promoting the Boot Camp Sweepstakes. Grand prize was a trip to Club Med. Also, Certs multipacks carried free packages of new Mini Mints and an in-pack Boot Camp Survival Guide, an irreverent "how-to" for budding comedians.

Local marketing support was focused in 15 markets where radio promotions were secured in return for grand prize trips to Club Med.

RESULTS

This integrated marketing program spanned eight months and elevated the brand's marketing efforts beyond "one-shot deals" as it preempted competition in the breath mints category with these results:
- Displays were obtained in 100,000 stores nationwide for the two events.
- More than $1 million in unpaid media were secured from radio promotions.
- More than $400,000 in donations were generated for Comic Relief.

Qualitatively, the Certs comedy campaign did indeed contemporize the brand and helped reach a new target audience of young consumers.

1992-93

CAMPAIGN/EVENT

Talkin' Can Sweepstakes

COMPANY

Coors Brewing Company

BRAND

Coors Light

YEAR

1992-93

BACKGROUND/MARKETING SITUATION

In 1992, Anheuser-Busch led the beer industry, but Miller was hot on its heels. Coors Light ran a distant third in sales in the premium beer category and second, behind Miller Lite, in the light beer segment.

Coors Light was also known to its 21 to 35 year old consumers as the Silver Bullet. The brand was at least as popular for its image as for its quality.

The beer industry was evolving. The marketing focus had shifted in recent months. In-store marketing, primarily consumer promotion and deep price cuts, was beginning to supplant advertising. In this environment, Coors competed with a distribution network that had to be shared with multiple brands, while the larger competition was able to offer dedicated delivery to retailers with focused field execution.

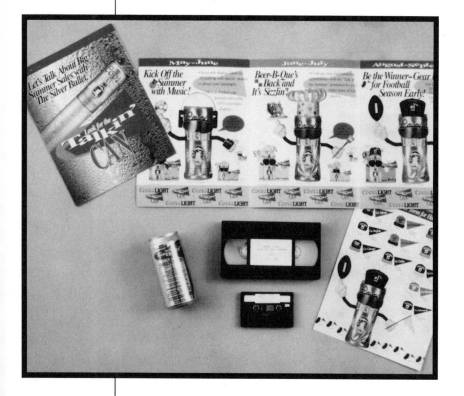

OBJECTIVES

Coors first needed to inspire its distributors to perform above their norm. Even more critical to success, because access to the retailers was difficult, for a Coors promotion to work, it necessitated introducing a definitive point of difference in the minds of consumers whose peremptory call to action hopefully would force trade compliance.

Thus, Coors objectives targeted consumers, and any trade program was confined to a supporting role:

- Motivate consumer purchase at off-premise retail.
- Secure features and displays during the key Memorial Day, July Fourth, and Labor Day weeks.

- Generate trial or retrial among new or occasional users.
- Enhance Coors Light brand positioning.
- Generate increments in both volume and in-store merchandising support.
- Maintain continuity throughout advertising, display, and promotion for exposure and media awareness.
- Off-set programming costs with tie-ins and trade-out of merchandise.
- Integrate Coors sales, marketing, and communications resources around a common goal.

PROGRAM/STRATEGY

Coors researched and developed the Talkin' Can to elicit sustained consumer interest throughout the 16-week promotional window from Memorial Day to Labor Day. It took 18 months and numerous trials before a can was refined to be indiscernible from actual Coors cans filled with beer. In the end, more than 40,000 seeded cans, when opened, triggered a light-activated voice chip that told consumers which of four levels of prizes they had won.

Talkin' Cans were featured in the three separate holiday executions:

- The Memorial Day theme focused on popular music and introduced music-related prizes. These prizes were used throughout the three executions.
- The July Fourth theme expanded music into the Coors Light Beer-B-Q Cookout.
- For Labor Day, a football theme featured a "dancing can" display and dancing can display decoration kits for depicting local professional and college football team colors.

There were four levels of prizes, ranging from 40,000 CDs or cassettes by top artists to 15 Denon Surround Sound Audio Systems. Any top-tier prize could be claimed by calling a toll-free number printed on the side of the can. Consumers who won cassettes or CDs (their choice) could pick from an assortment of Capitol Records top artists at Sam Goody or at Musicland. Coors negotiated prizes in return for mentions on cans, at point of purchase, on radio and TV. Tie-in partners included Capitol Records, Denon, Sam Goody-Musicland, and Koss. The total prize structure was valued at $1 million.

Support Activities included three :30 TV commercials, a :60 radio commercial, and three holiday tags. Sell-in materials were mailed in January, then Talkin' Cans were given to national accounts and distributors for their own key accounts. Point-of-purchase materials were produced in English and in Spanish.

RESULTS

The Talkin' Can Sweepstakes broke new ground by providing an intrusive in-pack promotion delivery device. Its enthusiastic reception by the public earned it over 40 interviews and articles in all media, the equivalent of 35 million gross impressions.

Reports from the field maintained that competitors had deepened their price discounting and had added refunds to remain competitive. Post-promotion research revealed that Talkin' Can awareness and recall were the highest of all brewery promotions, indexing higher than Bud Bowl and the Budweiser Summer Olympics. The success of this promotion enabled Coors to remain competitive with the brewing giants throughout the most important selling period of the year.

INDEX 1

This book's organization has one unique feature: Index 1. Unlike traditional indexes, it is organized as a product-promotion grid. The grid lists the winners down the left-hand margin. Across the top are the various kinds of promotion marketing techniques. For each promotion, the techniques used are listed, with the primary technique so indicated. The effect of the whole is to provide a highly usable "snapshot" of all techniques employed over the years, and their relative importance in overall promotion programs.

1983-84 PRODUCT

PRODUCT	CONSUMER	TRADE	FREE STANDING INSERT (FSI)	COUPON	GAMES/CONTESTS	SWEEPSTAKES	POINT OF SALE (POS)	PUBLIC RELATIONS/PUBLICITY	DIRECT MAIL
YAHAMA RIVA MOTORSCOOTER/ADIDAS	■					■ (primary)	■		
COCA-COLA	■						■		
BUSCH BEER	■				■ (primary)	■	■		
BUDWEISER BEER	■							■	
DEL MONTE CANNED AND PROCESSED FOODS	■								
TIDY CAT³ KITTY LITTER	■	▲			■ (primary)	▲			
GE VIDEOS	■					■ (primary)	■		
TIMBERLAND BOOTS	■					■ (primary)	■ ▲		
WHO KILLED THE ROBINS FAMILY? A NOVEL	■				■ (primary)		■	■	
REVLON FALL COSMETIC SHADES	■					■ (primary)	■		

 = consumer

▲ = trade

● = employee/sales force

 = technique used for both consumer & trade markets

 = primary vehicle

REFUNDS/ALLOWANCES	SAMPLING/PRODUCT DEMONSTRATION	PREMIUMS/INCENTIVES	CONTINUITY	EVENT/CHARITABLE CAUSE	TV	RADIO	PRINT	TRAINING FILM/VIDEO	TELEMARKETING	OTHER
							■			
■					■		■			
							■		■	
		■					■			
		■	■							
							■			
		●			■		■			
							■			
					■		■			

This grid may include elements that are not addressed in the summaries in this book but were part of the entries submitted for Reggie judging. In such summaries, elaboration by the editors on all specifics were constrained by either space or confidentiality. Likewise, the editors recognize that some elements of programs may have been omitted in the entries. Therefore, those familiar with the programs may find some elements missing on this grid.

1983-84
PRODUCT
(CONTINUED)

PRODUCT	CONSUMER	TRADE	FREE STANDING INSERT (FSI)	COUPON	GAMES/CONTESTS	SWEEPSTAKES	POINT OF SALE (POS)	PUBLIC RELATIONS/PUBLICITY	DIRECT MAIL
McDonald's restaurants	■						■		
MCI services	■		■▬	■					
B&B liqueur	■						■▬		
Orville Redenbacher's popcorns and popping oil	■	▲					■▬		
S&H Green Stamps	■			■					■▬
Scott tissue		▲				● ▲			

■ = consumer ■▲ = technique used for both consumer & trade markets

▲ = trade ●■▲ = primary vehicle

● = employee/sales force

REFUNDS/ALLOWANCES	SAMPLING/PRODUCT DEMONSTRATION	PREMIUMS/INCENTIVES	CONTINUITY	EVENT/CHARITABLE CAUSE	TV	RADIO	PRINT	TRAINING FILM/VIDEO	TELEMARKETING	OTHER
		■	■		■	■				
		■								
										Trade guests at movie screening
		■				■	■			
		●■▲								

This grid may include elements that are not addressed in the summaries in this book but were part of the entries submitted for Reggie judging. In such summaries, elaboration by the editors on all specifics were constrained by either space or confidentiality. Likewise, the editors recognize that some elements of programs may have been omitted in the entries. Therefore, those familiar with the programs may find some elements missing on this grid.

1984-85

PRODUCT	CONSUMER	TRADE	FREE STANDING INSERT (FSI)	COUPON	GAMES/CONTESTS	SWEEPSTAKES	POINT OF SALE (POS)	PUBLIC RELATIONS/PUBLICITY	DIRECT MAIL
McDonald's corporation	■				■ (primary)		■		
Michelob beer	■				■ (primary)		■		
Orville Redenbacher's popcorns and popping oil	■		■	■	■ (primary)		■		
Maxwell House instant coffee	■			■			■		■
Campbell's condensed soups	■		■		■	■ (primary)	■		
A&W root beer	■	▲					■ (primary)	▲	
Ziplock sandwich bags	■	▲	■	■			■		
7-Up	■	▲	■	■	■ (primary)		■		
Conrail railways		▲							▲ (primary)

 = consumer

▲ = trade

● = employee/sales force

 = technique used for both consumer & trade markets

●■▲ = primary vehicle

REFUNDS/ALLOWANCES	SAMPLING/PRODUCT DEMONSTRATION	PREMIUMS/INCENTIVES	CONTINUITY	EVENT/CHARITABLE CAUSE	TV	RADIO	PRINT	TRAINING FILM/VIDEO	TELEMARKETING	OTHER
			■							
							■			
▲			■		■					proof of purchase with entry
		■	■		■		■			free on-pack
		■	■		■	■	■			act media outdoor on-pack
▲		■ ▲			■	■	■			
▲		■	■		■		■			free on-pack
		■ ▲			■	■	■	▲		
		▲								research questionnaire

This grid may include elements that are not addressed in the summaries in this book but were part of the entries submitted for Reggie judging. In such summaries, elaboration by the editors on all specifics were constrained by either space or confidentiality. Likewise, the editors recognize that some elements of programs may have been omitted in the entries. Therefore, those familiar with the programs may find some elements missing on this grid.

1985-86 PRODUCT

PRODUCT	CONSUMER	TRADE	FREE STANDING INSERT (FSI)	COUPON	GAMES/CONTESTS	SWEEPSTAKES	POINT OF SALE (POS)	PUBLIC RELATIONS/PUBLICITY	DIRECT/M...
Cap'n Crunch cereal	■	▲	■		■ (primary)		■ ▲	■	
Contac cold medicine	■	▲		■		■ (primary) ▲	■	■	
Lays, Ruffles, O'Grady's potato chips	■	▲		■ ▲	■ (primary)	■ ▲	■ ▲		
Castrol GTX motor oil	■	▲					■ ▲		
Del Monte multibrand food product promotion	■	▲		■ ▲		■ (primary)	■		
Wilkinson disposable razors	■	▲	■				■		■
Mattel toys	■	▲			■ (primary)		▲	■	
Alka-Seltzer	■	▲		■		■ (primary) ▲	■ ▲		

■ = consumer

▲ = trade

● = employee/sales force

■ ▲ = technique used for both consumer & trade markets

●＿ ■＿ ▲＿ = primary vehicle

REFUNDS/ALLOWANCES	SAMPLING/PRODUCT DEMONSTRATION	PREMIUMS/INCENTIVES	CONTINUITY	EVENT/CHARITABLE CAUSE	TV	RADIO	PRINT	TRAINING FILM/VIDEO	TELEMARKETING	OTHER
		■			■	■	■			video, sunday comics
▲ ■ ▲		■			■					
									■	
■ ▬		■			■	■				
■										proofs-of-purchase
■ ▲	■ ▬									
										sunday comics, proofs-of-purchase

This grid may include elements that are not addressed in the summaries in this book but were part of the entries submitted for Reggie judging. In such summaries, elaboration by the editors on all specifics were constrained by either space or confidentiality. Likewise, the editors recognize that some elements of programs may have been omitted in the entries. Therefore, those familiar with the programs may find some elements missing on this grid.

1986-87 PRODUCT

PRODUCT	CONSUMER	TRADE	FREE STANDING INSERT (FSI)	COUPON	GAMES/CONTESTS	SWEEPSTAKES	POINT OF SALE (POS)	PUBLIC RELATIONS/PUBLICITY	DIRECT MAIL
MILLER LITE beer	■	▲			■ (primary)	■	■	■	
APPLE IIGS computer	■					■		■	
ALKA-SELTZER	■	▲	■	■			■		
7-UP	■	▲	■	■		■	■	■ ▲	
BRITISH AIRWAYS AIR TRAVEL	■	▲			■ (primary)	■	■	■	▲
ARMOR ALL AUTOMOTIVE FINISH PROTECTORS	■	▲			■ (primary) ▲		■		
ELF/ANTAR PETROLEUM PRODUCTS	■				■ (primary)		■		■
SHERATON HOTEL LOUNGES	■						■ (primary)		
PEPSI COLA MULTIPLE BRANDS	■			■			■		
DIET DR PEPPER	■	▲		■ ▲			■	■	

■ = consumer

▲ = trade

● = employee/sales force

■ ▲ = technique used for both consumer & trade markets

 = primary vehicle

REFUNDS/ ALLOWANCES	SAMPLING/ PRODUCT DEMONSTRATION	PREMIUMS/ INCENTIVES	CONTINUITY	EVENT/ CHARITABLE CAUSE	TV	RADIO	PRINT	TRAINING FILM/VIDEO	TELEMARKETING	OTHER
					■	■	■	●		
▲							▲			
	■	■		■		■	■			in-mall merchandising
■		■			■		■			
		▲								
		■		■	■	■	■			
							▲			
							■			outdoor
					■	■	■			
							■			
		▲								
		■	■		■	■				proofs-of-purchase
	■				■	■	■		■	
							▲			

This grid may include elements that are not addressed in the summaries in this book but were part of the entries submitted for Reggie judging. In such summaries, elaboration by the editors on all specifics were constrained by either space or confidentiality. Likewise, the editors recognize that some elements of programs may have been omitted in the entries. Therefore, those familiar with the programs may find some elements missing on this grid.

1987-88 PRODUCT

PRODUCT	CONSUMER	TRADE	FREE STANDING INSERT (FSI)	COUPON	GAMES/CONTESTS	SWEEPSTAKES	POINT OF SALE (POS)	PUBLIC RELATIONS/PUBLICITY	DIRECT MAIL
PEPSI COLA SOFT DRINKS MULTIPLE BRANDS	■	▲		■ ▲		■ (primary) ▲	■		
MAXWELL HOUSE COFFEES	■			■			■	■	
MILLER GENUINE DRAFT BEER	■					■ (primary)	■		
WISK DETERGENT	■	▲	■	■		■		■	
JOHNSON & JOHNSON HEALTH AND BEAUTY AIDS MULTIPLE BRANDS	■		■	■			■	■	
NIKE ATHLETIC FOOTWEAR	■	▲			■ (primary)	▲	■		
HARDEE'S RISE & SHINE BISCUITS AND DESSERTS	■						■		
FOOD WORLD, INC. GROCERY PRODUCTS	■			■			■		■
McDONALD'S McDLT SANDWICH	■ (primary)		■		■ (primary)		■	■	

■ = consumer
▲ = trade
● = employee/sales force
■ ▲ = technique used for both consumer & trade markets
● ■ ▲ = primary vehicle

REFUNDS/ALLOWANCES	SAMPLING/PRODUCT DEMONSTRATION	PREMIUMS/INCENTIVES	CONTINUITY	EVENT/CHARITABLE CAUSE	TV	RADIO	PRINT	TRAINING FILM/VIDEO	TELEMARKETING	OTHER
					■	■	■	●		ad on video
	■	■			■		■			
					■		■		■	
								▲		
▲				■	■	■	■			fireworks outdoor
				■	■	■	■		■	
	■					■	■			electronic phaser guns
		■ ●			■	■	■			outdoor local merchandising
■		■	■	■	■		■			buyers' club
					■	■	■			

This grid may include elements that are not addressed in the summaries in this book but were part of the entries submitted for Reggie judging. In such summaries, elaboration by the editors on all specifics were constrained by either space or confidentiality. Likewise, the editors recognize that some elements of programs may have been omitted in the entries. Therefore, those familiar with the programs may find some elements missing on this grid.

1988-89 PRODUCT

PRODUCT	CONSUMER	TRADE	FREE STANDING INSERT (FSI)	COUPON	GAMES/CONTESTS	SWEEPSTAKES	POINT OF SALE (POS)	PUBLIC RELATIONS/PUBLICITY	DIRECT MAIL
SEAGRAMS WINE COOLERS	■	▲					■	■▬	
MENNEN SPEED STICK DEODORANTS AND BABY MAGIC PRODUCTS	■	▲	■	■			■	■	
LEVER BROTHERS BAR SOAPS	■	▲	■	■	■▬	■	■	■	■
DENNY'S RESTAURANTS	■						■	■ ▲	■ ●
VICKERS GASOLINE	■			■			■	■ ▲	
KRAFT BULL'S-EYE BARBECUE SAUCE AND AMERICA'S CUT PORK	■			■			■		
FRISKIES DRY AND CANNED PET FOODS MULTIPLE BRANDS	■	▲	■	■			■		■
CITICORP SAVINGS FINANCIAL SERVICES	■						■ ▲	■▬ ▲	■
COCA-COLA CLASSIC	■	▲	■			■	■ ▲	■	
REPUBLIC NEW YORK FINANCIAL SERVICES	■						■▬	■	■

■ = consumer

▲ = trade

● = employee/sales force

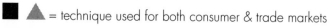
■ ▲ = technique used for both consumer & trade markets

● ■ ▲ = primary vehicle

REFUNDS/ALLOWANCES	SAMPLING/PRODUCT DEMONSTRATION	PREMIUMS/INCENTIVES	CONTINUITY	EVENT/CHARITABLE CAUSE	TV	RADIO	PRINT	TRAINING FILM/VIDEO	TELEMARKETING	OTHER
■ ▲		■ ▲	■	■ ▲	■		■	● ▲		
				■ ▲	■	■	■	▲		sales presentation support
■						■		● ▲		
		■	■	■	■	■	■			
				■	■	■	■			outdoor
	■						■			
		■ ▲		■			■		■	database marketing
		●					●	●		
		■ ▲		■	■	■	■	▲		
		■								

This grid may include elements that are not addressed in the summaries in this book but were part of the entries submitted for Reggie judging. In such summaries, elaboration by the editors on all specifics were constrained by either space or confidentiality. Likewise, the editors recognize that some elements of programs may have been omitted in the entries. Therefore, those familiar with the programs may find some elements missing on this grid.

1989-90 PRODUCT

PRODUCT	CONSUMER	TRADE	FREE STANDING INSERT (FSI)	COUPON	GAMES/CONTESTS	SWEEPSTAKES	POINT OF SALE (POS)	PUBLIC RELATIONS/PUBLICITY	DIRECT MAIL
CBS/KMART	■	▲	■		■ (primary) ●		■	■	■
MATTEL TOYS MULTIPLE BRANDS	■	▲		■			■	■ ▲	
EAGLE ELECTRICAL PRODUCTS		▲			▲	▲	▲		▲
PRODIGY COMPUTER SERVICES	■				■ (primary)				■
McDONALD'S NON-HAMBURGER ITEMS	■		■ (primary)	■	■	■	■	■	
VISA FINANCIAL SERVICES	■	▲				■ (primary)	■	▲	■
DIET COKE	■						■		
KRAFT FOODS MULTIPLE BRANDS	■	▲					■		
BANK SOUTH FINANCIAL SERVICES AND KROGER RETAIL FOODS	■								
BURGER KING MULTIPLE ITEMS	■						■		■ ▲

■ = consumer

▲ = trade

● = employee/sales force

■ ▲ = technique used for both consumer & trade markets

● ■ ▲ = primary vehicle

REFUNDS/ALLOWANCES	SAMPLING/PRODUCT DEMONSTRATION	PREMIUMS/INCENTIVES	CONTINUITY	EVENT/CHARITABLE CAUSE	TV	RADIO	PRINT	TRAINING FILM/VIDEO	TELEMARKETING	OTHER	
					■	■		■ ●			local events outdoor
■		■		■ ▬			■ ▲				local events
		● ▲	▲ ▬						▲		business to business
											computer billboard
		■			■	■					
					■	■	■	● ▲			statement stuffers
		■			■ ▬	■	■				3-D element
		■ ▬ ▲									
■ ▬		●	■		■	■	■				outdoor
		■	■ ▬		■						newsletter database

This grid may include elements that are not addressed in the summaries in this book but were part of the entries submitted for Reggie judging. In such summaries, elaboration by the editors on all specifics were constrained by either space or confidentiality. Likewise, the editors recognize that some elements of programs may have been omitted in the entries. Therefore, those familiar with the programs may find some elements missing on this grid.

1990-91 PRODUCT

PRODUCT	CONSUMER	TRADE	FREE STANDING INSERT (FSI)	COUPON	GAMES/CONTESTS	SWEEPSTAKES	POINT OF SALE (POS)	PUBLIC RELATIONS/PUBLICITY	DIRECT MAIL
RAINBOW FOODS — RETAIL	■						■	■	■
PILLSBURY MULTIPLE PRODUCTS	■	▲	■	■	▲	■ (primary)	■	■	▲
KRAFT CHEESE SINGLES	■		■	■	■ (primary)		■	■	■
COCA-COLA MULTIPLE PRODUCTS	■	▲			■ (primary)		■		
MILLER GENUINE DRAFT BEER	■				■ (primary)	■	■	■	
GILLETTE RIGHT GUARD DEODORANT	■					■ (primary)	■	■	
COLGATE TOOTHPASTE MULTIPLE AND LISTERINE MOUTHWASH MULTIPLE	■	▲	■ (primary)	■			■		
PIZZA HUT MULTIPLE ITEMS	■		■	■		■	■	■	■
MONSANTO LAWN & GARDEN PRODUCTS		▲			▲ (primary)	▲	▲		
NINTENDO COMPUTER GAMES	■	▲				■	■	■	■

■ = consumer

▲ = trade

● = employee/sales force

■ ▲ = technique used for both consumer & trade markets

● ■ ▲ = primary vehicle

REFUNDS/ALLOWANCES	SAMPLING/PRODUCT DEMONSTRATION	PREMIUMS/INCENTIVES	CONTINUITY	EVENT/CHARITABLE CAUSE	TV	RADIO	PRINT	TRAINING FILM/VIDEO	TELEMARKETING	OTHER
		■	■			■	■			
		■ ▲			■		■			
		▲			■	■	■	▲		sunday comics
					■	■				
		■			■	■		▲		
					■	■	■		■	
		■			■					bilingual support materials
		■	■	■	■	■	■			cable, local events
		▲							▲	
	■	■		■	■	■	■		■	sponsor tie-ins

This grid may include elements that are not addressed in the summaries in this book but were part of the entries submitted for Reggie judging. In such summaries, elaboration by the editors on all specifics were constrained by either space or confidentiality. Likewise, the editors recognize that some elements of programs may have been omitted in the entries. Therefore, those familiar with the programs may find some elements missing on this grid.

1991-92 PRODUCT

PRODUCT	CONSUMER	TRADE	FREE STANDING INSERT (FSI)	COUPON	GAMES/CONTESTS	SWEEPSTAKES	POINT OF SALE (POS)	PUBLIC RELATIONS/PUBLICITY	DIRECT MAIL
7-Eleven	■						■ (primary)	■	
Shopko retail merchandise	■				■	■	■		■
Western Union money transfers	■						■		
Campbell Soup Company multiple products	■	▲	■ (primary)	■			■		▲
Hallmark/Crayola	■	▲			■	■	■	■	
SuperAmerica gas and convenience stores	■	▲		■		■ (primary)	■		
NutraSweet	■		■			■ (primary)			
Maalox antacid	■	▲	■	■	■		■ ▲		
Leaf candy and gum multiple brands	■							■	■
ABC "General Hospital"	■				■ (primary)				

 = consumer

▲ = trade

● = employee/sales force

  = technique used for both consumer & trade markets

● ■ ▲ = primary vehicle

REFUNDS/ALLOWANCES	SAMPLING/PRODUCT DEMONSTRATION	PREMIUMS/INCENTIVES	CONTINUITY	EVENT/CHARITABLE CAUSE	TV	RADIO	PRINT	TRAINING FILM/VIDEO	TELEMARKETING	OTHER
			■			■	■			opinion poll
		▤			■	■				interactive display
		▤●			■	■	■			outdoor, mass transit
▲		▲								
		■		▤	■		■			
					■	■	■			
		▲						▲	■	
	■	■		■		▤				local events
	■		▤	■			■	■		database marketing
					■	▤				local events

This grid may include elements that are not addressed in the summaries in this book but were part of the entries submitted for Reggie judging. In such summaries, elaboration by the editors on all specifics were constrained by either space or confidentiality. Likewise, the editors recognize that some elements of programs may have been omitted in the entries. Therefore, those familiar with the programs may find some elements missing on this grid.

1992-93 PRODUCT

PRODUCT	CONSUMER	TRADE	FREE STANDING INSERT (FSI)	COUPON	GAMES/CONTESTS	SWEEPSTAKES	POINT OF SALE (POS)	PUBLIC RELATIONS/PUBLICITY	DIRECT MAIL
BARQ'S ROOT BEER	■	▲					■		
DORITOS	■	▲		■			■	■	
CRAYOLA	■	▲	■ (primary)	■	■	■	■		
EMERY BUSINESS-TO-BUSINESS FREIGHT		▲					▲		●
GATORADE DRINK AND FOOTLOCKER retail shoe stores	■	▲	■	■ (primary)			■	■	
KEYSTONE BEER	■						■	■	■
MEMTEK audio/video tape	■	▲			■ (primary)		■		▲
NATWEST financial services	■					■ (primary)	■		■
CERTS BREATH MINTS	■	▲				■	■		●, ▲
COORS LIGHT BEER	■	▲				■ (primary), ▲	■		

■ = consumer

▲ = trade

● = employee/sales force

■ ▲ = technique used for both consumer & trade markets

● ■ ▲ = primary vehicle

REFUNDS/ALLOWANCES	SAMPLING/PRODUCT DEMONSTRATION	PREMIUMS/INCENTIVES	CONTINUITY	EVENT/CHARITABLE CAUSE	TV	RADIO	PRINT	TRAINING FILM/VIDEO	TELEMARKETING	OTHER
		▣			■	■	■			
	▣ ●					■	■			
	■	■					▲			
▲		● ▲								
■	■	▲			■	■	■			
■		■				■	■		▣	
		■								
								▲		personnel training seminar
		■ ▲		▣	■	■	■	●		
		▲			■	■	▲		■	

This grid may include elements that are not addressed in the summaries in this book but were part of the entries submitted for Reggie judging. In such summaries, elaboration by the editors on all specifics were constrained by either space or confidentiality. Likewise, the editors recognize that some elements of programs may have been omitted in the entries. Therefore, those familiar with the programs may find some elements missing on this grid.

INDEX 2

INDEX 2

INDEX 2

INDEX 2

INDEX 2

INDEX 2

INDEX 2

INDEX 2

INDEX 2

INDEX

ABOUT THE EDITORS

Fran Caci is a Partner in Promotional Resources Group, Inc. (PRG). Fran has over 25 years' experience in the promotion industry on both the manufacturer and the agency side. Just prior to her association with PRG, Fran was Vice President of the American Consulting Corporation. The combination of corporate and agency background has provided Fran with firsthand experience on an extremely diverse number of brands. Her experience in the industry has qualified her as a judge on the Reggie Judging Committee on which she has been active for several years. Fran is also Vice-Chair of PMAA and has served on the Board of Directors of the PMAA since 1984.

Donna Howard began her promotion career as a packaged goods copywriter and graphic artist for a small agency in Long Island. Her first nuts–and–bolts turnkey event was a sweepstakes for New York's largest dealer in mail-order motorcycle parts and accessories. She later held successive positions in marketing management for an international children's aid federation and for a Connecticut real estate company. This was followed by several years as promotions development manager for Boyle Midway Household Products, when it was a division of American Home Products. In 1990, when Boyle Midway was sold and its promotion department dismantled, she joined Promotional Resources Group as Senior Account Executive.

YOUR KEYS TO MARKETING PROMOTION SUCCESS

Big Profits from Small Budget Advertising

by Herschell Gordon Lewis

250-Page Text; 125-Page Workshop; 3-Ring Binder; $91.50

More sales and profits on a smaller budget. Everybody wants that. Now you can have it in these 250 pages of easy-to-use guidelines:

● Position your product for profit
● Get the most from suppliers
● Buy the right media: radio/TV/print, Yellow Pages, direct mail, and more at the right price
● Make sense of the numbers
● Develop your own ad plan.

It's all here—plus a 100-page problem-solving Workshop to put these ideas into practice—and profit.

The Greatest Direct Mail Sales Letters of All Time

by Richard S. Hodgson
450-Page Text; 3-Ring Binder; $91.50

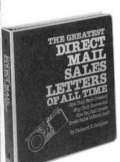

A leading authority in direct marketing today, Hodgson has compiled over 100 of the best sales letters ever written, each covering a wide variety of products and services. Each letter is presented in its entirety, then examined and analyzed by the author. Use or adapt these proven winners to reach your own particular objectives and goals.

Complete Guide to Catalog Marketing

by Richard S. Hodgson

420-Page Text; 16-Page, 4-Color Portfolio; 32-Page Catalog Workshop; 3-Ring Binder; $91.50

Take advantage of Dick Hodgson's 30-plus years of catalog marketing expertise with this step-by-step comprehensive guide. You'll learn the keys to successful catalogs, including identifying profitable markets and developing winning plans; building and maintaining your database; and creating, designing, and producing catalogs to sell more products and earn more profits. The full-color Catalog Portfolio gives you 16 pages of covers and layouts that sell. Plus the Catalog Workshop gives you 32 pages of "first-things-first" and "last-chance" guidelines to plan and manage more efficiently.

Copywriting Secrets & Tactics

by Herschell Gordon Lewis
255-Page Text; 147-Page Copywriters Workshop; 3-Ring Binder; $91.50

Words can make a difference—especially when those words are selling your product. Whether you're writing or reviewing copy for direct mail, catalogs, or other print media, *Copywriting Secrets & Tactics* will enable you to turn your words into sales copy that will cut through the clutter and sell more products.

✂ -

To order in U.S. or Canada call: (800) 621-5463 or FAX us your order (312) 561-3801

YES! Send me the books I have checked.
I understand if I am not completely satisfied, I may return my purchase within 30 days for a full refund.

❑ Big Profits from Small Budget Advertising	$91.50	❑ Building Sales with Demographics and Psychographics	$29.95
❑ The Greatest Direct Mail Sales Letters of All Time	$91.50	❑ How to Write Powerful Catalog Copy	$49.95
❑ Complete Guide to Catalog Marketing	$91.50	❑ Integrated Advertising	$34.95
❑ Copywriting Secrets & Tactics	$91.50	❑ Direct Marketing Strategies and Tactics	$49.95
		❑ Marketing Manager's Handbook	$69.95

Name_____ Title_____

Company_____ Phone_____

Address_____ Signature_____

City_____ State_____ Zip_____

Signature and phone number required to process order.
Prices subject to change.

❑ Please send me a free catalog of all Dartnell products.

93-5501

Building Sales with Demographics and Psychographics
by Judith E. Nichols
289 Pages; Hardcover; $29.95

Demographics. Psychographics. Buzzwords or Sales Builders? *Building Sales with Demographics and Psychographics* shows you how to cut through the "jargon," make the numbers work for you, and build your business with better marketing focus. Learn how to build your database by understanding basic customer characteristics, measuring attitudes and lifestyles, and how to expand and target your marketing to Baby Boomers, the Hispanic Majority, Aging America, Working Women, and Baby Busters by better understanding the psyche of each group. You'll get the numbers and statistics, but more importantly, you'll get the guidance to use them profitably.

How to Write Powerful Catalog Copy
by Herschell Gordon Lewis
331 Pages; Hardcover; $49.95

Herschell Gordon Lewis, columnist and feature writer for *Catalog Age* and *Direct Marketing* magazine, lays out solid principles for making catalog copy pull—then loads page after page with examples showing how to do it (and how not to do it). Each chapter begins with an exercise challenging you to solve a basic copywriting problem and then gives you the expert guidance to solve it in creative, sales-building, cost-effective ways. You'll learn how to write copy to establish the image of your catalog; clarify your product descriptions—while increasing sales purchases—and provide details the reader needs to buy your product. Plus, Lewis provides a list of 20 questions you should ask yourself before sending copy out the door, and 29 rules to writing successful catalog copy that will turn any novice into a superstar and the journeyman into a hero.

Integrated Advertising
by Carol Nelson
213 Pages; Hardcover; $34.95

Combine the long-term, image-building power of successful advertising with the here-and-now, profit potential of database and direct marketing in integrated advertising campaigns that work for both the short and long term. Loaded with illustrated checklists of pitfalls to avoid and new ways to identify your audience, harnessing data power for bigger profits. Hundreds of problem-solving ideas.

Direct Marketing Strategies and Tactics
by Herschell Gordon Lewis
370 Pages; Hardcover; $49.95

Put yourself on the inside track to profits in direct marketing—knowing how to use all the forms of direct marketing to squeeze the highest possible response from your programs. And this is the complete guide to learning how to:
- Target markets and customers
- Pick the right media
- What to "learn" from tests
- Use order cards, envelopes, and follow-up phone calls to increase response.

Plus 170 "impact ideas" you can put into practice today.

Marketing Manager's Handbook; 3rd Edition
1,293 Pages; Hardcover; $69.95

This classic handbook shows you how to establish realistic marketing objectives and reach them. 132 of the biggest names in marketing contributed to this volume.

✂ Clip and Mail This Order Form to:

The Dartnell Corporation
4660 N Ravenswood Ave
Chicago, IL 60640-4595

☎ For Faster Service Call:

U.S. and Canada: (800) 621-5463
FAX: (312) 561-3801